# FUN WITH PHONICS

# FUN WITH PHONICS

## English Phonics for Beginners

## Moi Hung Ling

PARTRIDGE

A Penguin Random House Company

**To order additional copies of this book, contact**
Toll Free 800 101 2657 (Singapore)
Toll Free 1 800 81 7340 (Malaysia)
orders.singapore@partridgepublishing.com

www.partridgepublishing.com/singapore

# Contents

# Preface

It is my belief that small children learn faster through listening / by hearing than reading the text. We all learn our mother tongue mostly through speech sounds. Children with normal hearing faculty learn the language (s) through hearing the speech sounds and connect them to the objects around them and concepts they relate to for meaning. Before they could express themselves to fulfil their needs, they code their language through listening and understanding the meaning.

Thus I see the value of songs, poems, limericks or any texts that provide the source for them to get familiar with the speech sounds. It does not matter if they do not quite understand the meaning of the songs they sing, the poems or limericks they hear. Let them enjoy the songs, poems or limericks for fun of the speech sounds they make and hear.

For older children, you may create the awareness of the letter clusters or the spelling for the specific speech sounds when reading texts are introduced to them. I see great value to teach phonics with some meaningful situations created to learn the regular spelling patterns with the specific speech sounds. This exposure will certainly help our children remember English words easily. When they know the basic letter clusters of the words, for example,

> 'ear', in 'bear, dear, hear, fear, gear, beard,
> pear, pearl, smear, near, spear, ..... ;
> 'air in chair, fair, flair, pair, stair, ......';
> 'are' in 'care, dare, fare, glare, hare, spare, declare,
> prepare.......'

they will find English spelling so easy to master.

Hence phonics help children or adults to see word(s) in a word. However, the same letter clusters may have different speech sounds, for example,

/ Iə / ear, hear, fear, gear, beard, smear, near, spear

/ eə / bear, pear, wear

/ ɜ: / earl, early, earth

Besides, reading aloud not only helps children become familiar with the speech sounds but also intonation patterns.

Well, I hope this book will prove to be useful to those who are eager to learn English basic speech sounds, intonation patterns and the spelling at ease.

# Vowels

| No. | Phonemes | Helping Words |
|-----|----------|---------------|
| 1. | / i: / | E |
| 2. | / I / | **it** |
| | | |
| 3. | / eɪ / | A |
| 4. | / e / | egg |
| | | |
| 5. | / æ / | cat |
| | | |
| 6. | / ɑ: / | R |
| 7. | / ɒ / | dog |
| 8. | / ʌ / | up |
| | | |
| 9. | / u: / | blue |
| 10. | / ʊ / | book |
| | | |
| 11. | / əʊ / | O |
| 12. | / ɔ: / | awe |
| 13. | / 3: / | sir |
| 14. | / ə / (/ ə'gəʊ /) | ago |
| | | |
| 15. | / aɪ / | I |
| 16. | / aʊ / | cow |
| 17. | / ɔI / | oil |
| | | |
| 18. | / ɪ ə / | ear |
| 19. | / e ə / | air |
| 20. | / ʊə / | tour |

(ii)

Some dictionaries give second length of / i: / second with the symbol / i / for the letter 'y' ending in the words like 'happy, angry, ready....'. here, I only use / I / to replace / I / sound.

## 1. Vowel Phoneme / i: /

| Letter clusters | Phoneme | helping word | |
|---|---|---|---|
| [ ea, ee, eo, ie ] | / i: / | E | 1 – 12 |

S<u>ea</u>n lives by the s<u>ea</u>.

H<u>e</u> always gr<u>ee</u>ts the sea

with so much gl<u>ee</u>.

He always l<u>ea</u>ps

with so much joy

to s<u>ee</u> seagulls

flying high and low above the sea (/ si: /).

He likes to take the s<u>ea</u>t (/ si:t /) made of t<u>ea</u>k (/ ti:k /)

under a row of thr<u>ee</u> tr<u>ee</u>s

He likes to m<u>ee</u>t p<u>eo</u>ple (/ 'pi:pl /) by the s<u>ea</u>

and greet them with so much glee (/ gli: /).

| [ ea, ee ] | / iː / | E | 2 |
|---|---|---|---|

Sean likes to beat (/ biːt /) the drum

when he eats peas and beans.

He likes to eat leeks.

He eats meat once a week (/ wiːk /).

His mum needs to heat up the meat

before he eats.

He feels weak

when he does not eat leek for a week.

| [ ea, ee ] | / iː / | E | 3 |
|---|---|---|---|

Sean likes to read

when he is free (/ friː /).

He likes to sit in an easy chair

when he reads.

He always falls asleep (/ əˈsliːp /)

in an easy chair when he reads.

Mdm Chan, Sean's mum always pleads (pliːdz) him

to read at the desk.

Sean does not seem keen

to read in that way.

He feels more at ease (/ iːz /)

to read in an easy chair.

So he always falls asleep

in an easy chair when he reads.

| [ ea, ee ] | / iː / | E | 4 |
|---|---|---|---|

Sean always pleads,

"Tell me some stories, please. Dear mummy."

He pleads his mummy for some stories

before he sleeps.

"You may repeat (/ rI'piːt /) the same story,

'The Princess Sleeping on a Pea', please,"

he squeaks and squeals (skwiːlz) sometimes

when he is cranky.

| [ ea, ee ] | / i: / | E | 5 |
|---|---|---|---|

Sean likes to drink tea (/ ti: /)

like his teacher Anna Lee.

She always drinks tea

besides a heap of books, neat and clean (/ kli:n /).

She always chuckles reading the book

about a bird with a long big beak.

The bird likes to eat wheat

and feels at ease in a corner.

The wheat is cheap

and the farmer always gives it for a treat (/ tri:t /).

The farmer and the bird with a long big beak

always live in peace and at ease

At least the farmer never feels uneasy

with the bird with a long big beak.

| [ ea, ee ] | / i: / | E | 6 |
|---|---|---|---|

Sean likes to lead the class to read the book

about the bird with a long big beak.

He likes to highlight how the bees (/ bi:z /)

make the wheat (/ wi:t /) nice and sweet.

The bees sneak into the barn

when the farmer is not around.

They make the wheat sweet with honey.

The bird with a long big beak

likes to seek for some tree seeds (/ si:dz /)

he needs to make wheat-seed meal.

| [ ea, ee ] | / i: / | E | 7 |
|---|---|---|---|

The farmer likes to drive his jeep around.

He goes to his barn once a week.

He likes to peep into a hole to see

how his pet bird enjoys its wheat-seed meal.

The farmer uses a needle (/ ˈniːdl /) to clean

the peeping hole to peep in.

He knows how the bees make the wheat sweet.

The honey seeps into wheat slowly

to make it nice and sweet.

He knows how hard his pet bird

seek for the tree seeds

He knows how it sweeps off

the husks under the heap.

He takes a peek at the food.

He laughs sneakily to himself.

Wheat it eats is sweet indeed.

| [ ea, ee ] | / iː / | E | 8 |
|---|---|---|---|

The bird with a long big beak

seems so meek and sleepy

with wheat- seed meal.

It falls into a sweet, deep sleep

immediately after it.

The farmer nearly cries in grief

to see his pet bird lying so flat and stiff.

He heaves a sigh of relief (/ rɪˈliːf /)

when he realises (/ riːˈlaɪzəz /)

that his pet bird is only in a sweet deep sleep.

| [ ea, ee, ie ] | / iː / | E | 9 |
|---|---|---|---|

The bees in the field (fiːld) are dancing

with so much glee.

The chief of the bees is in the belief (bɪˈliːf)

that they should sieve (/ siːv /) the honey

which they yield (/ jiːld /).

They should shield (/ ʃiːld /) the beehive

to keep off a sneaky (ˈsniːkI) bear, the thief (/ θiːf /).

The chief (/ tʃiːf /) of the bees wields (/ wiːldz /) the power

to brief (briːf) the bees to keep the yield in a seal (/ siːl /).

| [ ea, ee, ie ] | / i: / | E | 10 |
| --- | --- | --- | --- |

Sean likes to eat ice-cream.

He screams (/ skri:mz /) for one

even in his dream

He often dreams about eating ice-cream

by the stream near the spring

which gives out so much steam.

| [ ea, ee, ie ] | / i: / | E | 11 |
| --- | --- | --- | --- |

Sean is a player in a football team.

He and his team always beam.

Their team coach Geo. B likes

to treat them with ice-cream

Sean always leaps and screams

to thank him for the ice-cream.

Team Coach George B likes to say,

"You reap(/ ri:p /) what you sow."

Sean leaps and screams even more.

He repeats the proverb

with his leader (/ ˈli:də(r) /) George B,

"You reap what you sow."

The two boys leap up really high

with a sharp loud scream.

They have a real (/ ri:l /)

and meaningful (/ ˈmi:ŋɪŋfl /) day in the field.

| [ ea, ee ] | / iː / | E | 12 |
|---|---|---|---|

Sean likes to eat durians

when they are in season (/ ˈsiːzn /).

He eats so many durians

with many good reasons (/ riːznz /).

When he becomes so heaty (/ ˈhiːtɪ /),

he eats a lot of ice-cream.

He also keeps his cheeks

and body cool with some cream.

## 2. Vowel Phoneme / I /

| Letters | phoneme | helping word | |
|---|---|---|---|
| [ i ] | / I / | it | |
| | / a I / | I | 13 – 22 |

Sean lives in a big house by (/ baI /) the sea.

He likes to go for a dip (/ dIp /) in the mid of the day.

He mixes around

He always invites his friends,

Bip, Jip, Nick and Tip to go for a swim.

They like to sing (sIŋ) when they swim.

They sink (sIŋk) when they stop singing.

They like to sit by the poolside

to sing and think (/ θIŋk /).

They think it fun to sit (/ sIt /)

in the sun to sing and think.

| [ i ] | / I /, / aɪ / | it, I | 14 |

Sean thinks that Bip is really thin (/ θɪn /).

He always carried a big tin (/ tɪn /)

when he goes for a swim.

He puts everything in the tin

and closes it with a lid

and locks it with a key (/ ki: /).

| [ i ] | / I /, / aI / | it, I | 15 |
|-------|---------------|-------|-----|

Jip is not thin.

He wants to be slim.

He believes he can be slim

when he always goes for a swim.

He likes to walk up the hill

with his brother, Bill.

He always feels ill (/ ɪl /) at ease

when he walks down the hill.

| [ i ] | / I /, / aI / | it, I | 16 |
|---|---|---|---|

Tip is not so thin, either (/ ˈaIðə(r) /). (/ ˈiːðə(r) /)

But he always looks so pink

He blinks and winks a lot

when he is sick  / sIk /.

He likes to go for a swim to keep fit.

He is always so happy

whenever he can go for a dip

to keep fit.

| [ i ] | / I /, / aI / | it, I | 17 |
|---|---|---|---|

Nick is a little bit fat.

He knows it.

He decides (/ dI'saIdz /) to reduce some weight.

He thinks swimming can help him

keep fit and slim.

He likes to flip (/ flIp /) in water.

He has to pinch (pIntʃ) his nose

and keeps his lips really tight (/ taIt /)

in the act of flipping in water.

He can do it for 2 minutes ('mInIts).

He feels delighted to do it.

Sean thinks himself is in between

Bip and Jip in weight (weIt) and height(/ haIt /).

| [ i ] | / I /, / aI / | it, I | 18 |

Sean, Bip, Jip, Nick and Tip have heard

the story about 5 fat women (/ 'wImən /).

One woman (/ 'wʊmən /) is really fat.

She is called Mick

She is at least 5 Nicks in weight.

and 2 Nicks in height.

Nick is only eight.

The woman is thirty plus eight.

She often slips and falls.

She needs the other four fat women (/ 'wImən /)

to lift (/ lIft /) her up to her feet (/ fi:t /).

| [ i ] | / I /, / aI / | it, I | 19 |
|---|---|---|---|

Mick has a really big hip.

She always goes for a trip (/ trIp /)

to town on a fine (/ faIn /) day.

But she always has a hard time (taIm)

to find a chair in town

where she can sit down to take a sip

before she goes for a dip.

| [ i ] | / I /, / aɪ / | it, I | 20 |
|---|---|---|---|

The five women Mick, Pik, Rick, Silk and Vick

are good friends.

They each (/ i:tʃ /) carry a walking stick.

They always walk about

with click-tick sounds.

Sometimes they grip the tip

of the sticks of one another.

They walk in a file (/ faɪl /) to form a link (/ lɪŋk /).

Sometimes they form a ring (rɪŋ)

to gossip or sing (/ sɪŋ /).

They make a lot of hissing (/ 'hɪsɪŋ /) sounds.

At times they all give hilarious (hɪ'leərɪəs) laugh.

Then they will sling (/ slɪŋ /) their walking sticks.

And they fall into hysterical (hɪ'sterɪkl) laugh.

They laugh and laugh until they turn stiff (/ stɪf /).

| [ i ] | / ɪ /, / aɪ / | it, I | 21 |
| --- | --- | --- | --- |

Vick has to prick (prɪk) them

to stop them laughing for a while (/ waɪl /).

Mick quickly takes out

the pickled ('pɪkld) lime to lick.

Her action tickles ('tɪklz) others

to laugh even more.

They are like practising

'laughing yoga' in a ring in public (/ 'pʌblɪk /).

| [ i ] | / I /, / aI / | it, I | 22 |
|---|---|---|---|

Some teenage boys and girls happen

to be beside (/ bI'saId /) them.

They are roaring into laughter

at the sight (saIt) of 5 fat women laughing hysterically.

Their mouths are wide (/ waId /) open

as big (/ bIg /) as a hippopotamus

when they laugh side by side

with so much delight (/ dI'laIt /).

The five fat women turn still and stiff

to hear roaring laughter beside them

They pick up their walking sticks

and take a brisk (/ brIsk /) walk away in a file (/ faIl /).

They are singing (/ 'sIŋIŋ /) in chorus

"A Happy Wander" side by side (/ saId /)

to go for some cool refreshing drinks

and then for a swim.

## 3. Minimal pairs: vowels varying in length / i: / Vs / I /

| | / i: / | / I / | 23 |
|---|---|---|---|
| 1. | eat | it | |
| 2. | beat | bit | |
| 3. | bead | bid | |
| 4. | been | bin | |
| 5. | deep | dip | |
| 6. | feat, feet | fit | |
| 7. | feel | fill | |
| 8. | green | grin | |
| 9. | heat | hit | |
| 10. | heap | hip | |
| 11. | heal | hill | |
| 12. | jeep | jip | |
| 13. | peat | pit | |
| 14. | peak | pick | |
| 15. | read | rid | |
| 16. | real | rill | |
| 17. | reap | rip | |
| 18. | seek | sick | |
| 19. | seal | sill | |
| 20. | seen | sin | |
| 21. | seat | sit | |
| 22. | sheep | ship | |
| 23. | sleep | slip | |
| 24. | teak | tick | |
| 25. | teen | tin | |
| 26. | week, weak | wick | |

4 Vowel Phoneme  /  eɪ  /

| Letters | Phoneme | Words | |
|---|---|---|---|
| [ ace, ade, afe, age, ail, ain, ake, ale, ame, ane, ape, ase, aste, ate ave, ay, ] | / eɪ / | A | 24 – 31 |

Sean washes his face (/ feɪs /) twice a day.

He thinks it is safe (/ seɪf /)

to use a little toothpaste

to brush his teeth twice a day.

He does not think it

a waste (/ weɪst /) of time or water

to bathe (beɪð) himself twice every day.

He always says it pays (peɪz)

to be clean and in grace (/ greɪs /).

He agrees with the saying,

"Cleanliness is next to holiness." (/ ˈhəulɪnəs /)

| [ ade, age, ain ange, ame, eight ] | / eɪ / | A | 25 |
| --- | --- | --- | --- |

Sean and his cousin, Sage are of the same age. (eɪdʒ)

They are aged eight (/ eɪt /)

and they are in Grade Three.

They like to sit under the shade (/ ʃeɪd /)

of a really big tree

Sage always carries a cage

with a parrot in it.

He always feeds it

with grains (greɪnz) and some orange.

Sean always carries a spade (/ speɪd /).

He wants to get some earthworms (/ 'ɜ:θwɜ:mz /)

to feed his goldfish at home.

| [ ade, ai, ay ] | / eɪ / | A | 26 |

When it r<u>ai</u>ns, Sean cannot w<u>ai</u>t (/ weɪt /) to go out

to w<u>a</u>de (/ weɪd /) in flooded water.

He likes to look into the dr<u>ai</u>ns (dreɪnz)

for some fishes or frogs.

He always carries along his toy tr<u>ai</u>n (/ treɪn /).

His father bought it for him

in the arc<u>a</u>de (/ ɑːˈkeɪd /) not far aw<u>ay</u> from his home.

He bought it on his w<u>ay</u> home one d<u>ay</u>

on Sean's birthday.

| age, ame, | / eɪ / | A | 27 |
|-----------|--------|---|-----|

Sean has many cousins.

One of them is named (/ neɪmd /) Page (/ peɪdʒ /).

Sean and Page are not of the same (/ seɪm /) age.

He came (/ keɪm /) last Sunday.

He has a dog named Dame.

He has another dog named Tame.

They look more or less the same (seɪm).

They always follow Page

wherever he goes.

| [ age, ai, ake, ame, ane ] | / eɪ / | A | 28 |
|---|---|---|---|

Page has kept a quail (/ kweɪl /)

named Faith (/ feɪθ /) in a cage.

Faith often wails in rage in protest.

Dame and Tame then wag their tails in contest.

This makes, Faith, the quail, fly into a rage. (reɪdʒ)

Page has to take up the cane

to stop the act of Dame and Tame.

Then they bow their heads

and howl in shame (/ ʃeɪm /).

[ ace, ade, ai, ake, ase, aste, ate, ay ]　　　/ eɪ /　　A　　29

It is Tip's birthday.

Sean wants to make a cake

to take (/ teɪk /) to his home.

Sean's mum has baked him a Horlick cake.

She has laced it with so much cake cream

and put it in a big case (/ keɪs /).

She has also made some paste.

Sean hates to be late to the birthday party.

He has dressed up in haste (/ heɪst /)

and is waiting for his mum at the gate.

He is carrying a big case of cake in one hand

and a bowl of paste in the other.

| [ age, ail ] | / eɪ / | A | 30 |

Sage's father has a dog named Hail.

It has a really long tail.

It never fails to follow

Sage's father to go for a sail (seɪl).

Sage's father always carries a pail

whenever he goes for a sail.

Hail always trails (/ treɪlz /)

beside his big blue pail.

| [ ake, ape ] | / eɪ / | A | 31 |

Sean likes to eat grapes.

He likes to eat grapes (greɪps)

and listen to the tape about an ape.

Sean thinks the ape has the shape (/ ʃeɪp /) of a man

and the nape of a chimpanzee (ˌtʃɪmpæn'ziː).

Sean always shakes (/ ʃeɪks /) his head

with his mouth agape

when he listens to the story about the ape (eɪp).

## 5 Vowel Phoneme / e /

| Letter(s) | Phoneme | Word | |
|-----------|---------|------|---|
| [ e ] | / e / | egg | 32 -- 38 |

Sean likes to sing the song, "To Be Happy".

His sister, Jean, always likes to sing along.

    To be happy, I eat well (/ wel /);

    I sleep well,

    I play and pray well.

    I work as well.

    I try everything (/ ˈevrɪθɪŋ /)

    to the best (/ best /) I can

    to be (/ biː /), to be, to be happy.

| [ e ] | / e / | egg | 33 |

Sean is sick in bed (/ bed /).

His face is really red.

His neck is red, too.

He eats so much less (/ les /).

He only wants an egg (/ eg /)

from the nest (/ nest /).

| [ e ] | / e / | egg | 34 |
|---|---|---|---|

There are quite many hens in the coop.

The coop is really in a mess (/ mes /).

Sean's mum wants to sell off all the hens.

She often tells Sean about the ten men

who mended the fence (/ fens /)

and how the hens pecked them.

She had to lend them umbrellas (ʌmˈbreləs)

to defend (/ dɪˈfend /) themselves

and shooed the hens away.

The ten men spent the whole afternoon

mending the fence (/ fens /)

and defending themselves (/ ðəmˈselvz /)

from the peck (pek) of those hens.

| [ e ] | / e / | egg | 35 |
|-------|-------|-----|-----|

Dr Vet, Sean's dad has a fishing net.

It is always wet (/ wet /).

He has a pet dog called Jet.

Jet wears a bell around its neck

It always gets excited

when the sun sets.

Dr Vet, Sean's dad lets it go out at sunset.

Jet will feel upset

if it does not go out at sunset.

Yesterday he nearly met (/ met /) with an accident.

when he went out to smell (/ smel /) around

and to meet his friends.

Jet was so frightened

that all his fur stood at its end.

| [ e ] | / e / | egg | 36 |
|-------|-------|-----|----|

Sean's dad is a vet.

He always wears a vest (/ vest /).

He likes to take a rest

at noon and at sunset.

He likes to take a rest (/ rest /)

in an easy chair

beside a chest of drawers

next to a desk.

He has a big shelf to his left (/ left /).

Nowadays he is so worried

about the different pests in his garden.

He feels rather restless

at the thought of all those pests.

| [ e ] | / e / | egg | 37 |
|-------|-------|-----|-----|

Sean has a friend called Hed.

He likes to eat bread (/ bred /).

He can eat a loaf of bread at one go.

He always has a headache (/ 'hedeɪk /)

if he does not have bread.

He is only eight

but he weighs (weɪz) seven times his age.

His height, well, is only one hundred

and twenty-seven (/ 'twentI /) (/ 'sevn /) in cm.

He is really heavy ('hevI).

Then Ted, Hed's dad, never hesitates to say,

"Son, you are overweight."

Hed's mum, Ned is upset, too.

She never hesitates to comment,

"Son, you are obese (/ əʊ 'biːs /)."

| [ e ] | / e / | egg | 38 |

Hed knows being obese is not good to his health. (/ helθ /)

He knows, "Health is more important than wealth." (/ welθ /)

He still remembers his dead (/ ded /) pet hamster, Wai-I.

It died of a heart attack being so fat.

Hed's mum, Ned and his dad, Ted want him

to get ready ('redɪ) for a weight loss.

They want him to eat less bread

and exercise more than Toss, their neighbour (/ 'neɪbə(r) /).

He always holds his toy weapon ('wepən)

and cries, "No! No!"

## 6. Minimal Pairs: / eɪ / Vs / e / Vowels varying in length

| | / eɪ / | / e / | 39 |
|---|---|---|---|
| 1. | bail | bell | |
| 2. | bait | bet | |
| 3. | fail | fell | |
| 4. | hail, hale | hell | |
| 5. | lace | less | |
| 6. | lane, lain | len | |
| 7. | late | let | |
| 8. | mane, main | men | |
| 9. | mate | met | |
| 10. | pane, pain | pen | |
| 11. | pate | pet | |
| 12. | paste | pest | |
| 13. | quail | quell | |
| 14. | raid | red | |
| 15. | sale | sell, cell | |
| 16. | sate | set | |
| 17. | tale | tell | |
| 18. | taste | test | |
| 19. | wait | wet | |

Do you have any more to add in?

## 7. Vowel Phoneme / æ /

| Letter(s) | Phoneme | Word | |
|---|---|---|---|
| [ a ] | / æ / | cat | 40 |

Hed felt bad and sad yesterday.

He felt mad (/ mæd /) as well

when his mum only gave (/ geɪv /)him

half a loaf of bread.

He sank (sæŋk) into the bean bag

and yank (jæŋk) off the head of his toy cat.

When his dad, Ted's pet kitty, Ann saw this,

she was really frightened.

She ran (ræn) really fast (/ f ɑːst /) for her life.

| [ a ] | / æ / | cat | 41 |
|-------|-------|-----|-----|

Hed has a toy van (væn).

He likes to play with it on the sand.

Ann quite likes Hed's toy van.

But she only stands (stændz) behind a tank

and looks at it.

Ann has a can and a pan

to play with behind the tank.

A pan and a can clank (klæŋk)

when Ann pushes the can into the pan.

| [ a ] | / æ / | cat | 42 |
| --- | --- | --- | --- |

Hed cannot have too much bread.

He has an apple instead.

He is not angry ('æŋgrI).

In fact, he feels glad to wear a black cap

and carries a small flag (/ flæg /).

He claps his hands when he sees a bat.

He taps his feet when he sees a rat.

He pats his shoulders

when he sees his neighbour's cat.

He dances to the tune of the music

when he sees the band (bænd).

He is no longer mad with so little bread.

| [ a ] | / æ / | cat | 43 |
|-------|-------|-----|----|

Hed also likes to wear a hat (/ hæt /).

He thinks wearing a hat

does not make him look so fat.

Sometimes he carries a map (/ mæp /)

and a bag on his back.

He packs a big floor mat in his bag.

He likes to take a nap on the mat

under an old big tree

near the grand (/ grænd /) old house.

## 8. Minimal Pairs / e / Vs / æ /

| | / e / | / æ / | 44 |
|---|---|---|---|
| 1. | bed | bad | |
| 2. | bet | bat | |
| 3. | Ben | ban | |
| 4. | bend | band | |
| 5. | lend | land | |
| 6. | send | sand | |
| 7. | fen | fan | |
| 8. | less | lass | |
| 9. | met | mat | |
| 10. | men | man | |
| 11. | peck | pack | |
| 12. | pen | pan | |
| 13. | pet | pat | |
| 14. | set | sat | |
| 15. | rent | rant | |
| 16. | cent | *cant | |
| 17. | ten | tan | |

Note:

No. 16 The words "cent and cant" are not considered as a minimal pairs because there are more than 2 speech sounds difference.

cent          / sent /          cant          / k æ nt /

## 9. Vowel Phoneme / ɑː /

| Letter(s) | Phoneme | Word | |
|---|---|---|---|
| [ a, ar ] | / ɑː / | are | 45 – 50 |

Sean's mum wants him to learn art (/ ɑːt /).

She wants him to work hard and be smart.

He has to learn the multiplication table by heart. (/ hɑːt /)

Sean then may go to the park

with a bar of chocolate and an egg tart (tɑːt).

Sean thinks his mum,

Mdm Chan is really obsessed with marks.

She even puts all his scores in a chart (/ tʃɑːt /).

| [ a, ar ] | / ɑ: / | car | 46 |

Sean always carries a basket of toy cars

when he goes to the park.

He brings along his mask (/ mɑ:sk /)

and a pack of cards.

He likes to put on his mask

to play cards with his friend, Mark.

Sean's father, Dr Vet's pet, Jet gets really excited

when he can go to the park, too.

He yelps and barks so much.

He runs really fast (/ fɑ:st /)

and always runs far ahead of Sean, his master.

When Sean calls Jet to slow down,

Jet seems to run many times faster.

Sean always thinks Jet

a hard nut in shell to crack (kræk).

Sean laughs and laughs (lɑ:fs) at the thought.

He almost drops the bar of chocolate

and the egg tart.

| [ a, ar ] | / ɑː / | car | 47 |

Sean's mum, Mdm Chan likes to take a sun bask

near a palm (/ p ɑːm /) tree in her garden (/ 'gɑːdn /).

She likes to apply some balm on her palm.

She wants to look calm and charmed (/ tʃɑːmd /).

She likes to take some almond nuts with sardines

and a jar (/ dʒɑː /) of grape juice

when she basks (/ bɑːsks /).

| [ a, ar ] | / ɑː / | car | 48 |

Mdm Chan always takes a b<u>a</u>th (/ bɑːθ /)

<u>a</u>fter (ɑːftə(r)) h<u>a</u>lf (hɑːf) an hour of sun b<u>a</u>sk.

She usually takes a bath (/ b ɑːθ /)

at h<u>a</u>lf p<u>a</u>st three in the afternoon.

When she takes a bath,

she st<u>ar</u>ts singing like a l<u>ar</u>k in the bath-tub.

Her voice is just too sharp (ʃɑːp).

She often startles the cocks

and hens in the coop

when she sings

at the top of her voice.

| [ a, ar ] | / ɑː / | car | 49 |
|---|---|---|---|

Mdm Chan goes to supermarket

once in a while.

She thinks all the goods

at the supermarket are charged (/ tʃɑːdʒd /)

at a fixed price.

She cannot bargain at all.

She always thinks it hard and harsh (/ hɑːʃ /)

when all the goods are charged

at a fixed price.

She thinks shopping

at a supermarket is a difficult task (/ tɑːsk /).

She always has to guard (/ gɑːd /)

against buying too much.

| [ a, ar ] | / ɑː / | car | 50 |
|---|---|---|---|

Sean likes to sit on the grass (/ grɑːs /)

drinking a glass of water

and a jar of fruit juice.

Jet, Dr Vet's pet likes to lie on his stomach ('stʌmək)

on the grass eating sardines (/ sɑːdɪnz /) and pizza.

Sean and Jet are happy to see the grasshoppers

hopping all over the place (pleɪs).

Jet always charges at them hoping

to catch (/ kætʃ /) some to eat with sardines and pizza.

## 10. Vowel Phoneme / ɒ /

| Letter(s) | Phoneme | Helping Word | |
|-----------|---------|--------------|---|
| [ o ] | / ɒ / | hot | 51 – 52 |

Dr Vet's pet dog, Jet likes to lie flat

besides a log (/ lɒg /).

At times, he likes to hop like a frog

when he plays with the hog.

Sometimes, he also tries to jog (/ dʒɒg /)

in the bog to show off.

Once in a while, Jet acts bossy (/ 'bɒsɪ /)

and stomps about like a cop.

But he always dodges to meet,

Dr Vet's pet donkey, Doss.

When they chance to meet,

he never bothers ('bɒðəz) to look at him.

He thinks he quite likes Dollox, the star dolphin ('dɒlfɪn).

He is friendly to Cox, the ox (/ ɒks /).

He always greets Cox, the ox happily.

| [ o ] | / ɒ / | hot | 52 |
|-------|-------|-----|-----|

The weather got really hot the other (/ ʌðə(r) /) day.

Jet, Dr Vet's pet dog, wanted to go (/ gəʊ /)

to a pond (pɒnd) for a swim.

Jet is fond of swimming in a pond.

It walked a long (lɒŋ) way to look

for the pond he has a bond.

It is near a lodge of somebody (/ ˈsʌmb ə dɪ /).

He found it after a long search.

He had a lot (/ lɒt /) of fun swimming around.

But he forgot the way home

He almost got lost in the bog.

and nearly got shot by a hunter

who mistook him to be a wild hog (/ hɒg /).

Jet yelped and barked to tell the hunter

he was actually somebody's pet dog.

## 11. Vowel Phoneme  / ^ /

| Letter(s) | Phoneme | Helping Word | |
|-----------|---------|--------------|--------|
| [ u, o, ou ] | / ^ / | up | 53 – 56 |

Mdm Chan, Sean's mum likes to sit down

when she does (/ dʌz /) some work.

But she always stands up

when she has to cut (/ kʌt /) meat.

She stands up

when she wants to take

a cup of tea or coffee.

She likes to stand beside the cupboard

where she puts all the cups and cutlery (kʌtlərɪ)

to eat some nuts (nʌts).

| [ o, u ] | / ʌ / | cut | 54 |

Mdm Chan, Sean's mum Keeps some ducks in a hut.

She always thinks it fun to see her ducks (/ dʌks /)

playing in the tub besides the hut (/ hʌt /).

She must keep the hut clean as such.

She always allocates some fund

to buy sawdust and rice husks

to suck the water in the hut.

Sean's mum always thinks herself

to have so much luck (/ lʌks /)

as she can keep so many ducks.

| [ o, u ] | / ʌ / | cut | 55 |
|----------|-------|-----|-----|

Sean's m<u>u</u>m always dusts, rubs

and scrubs the house on Monday (/ 'mʌndeɪ /).

She always get the work done (/ dʌn /)

before Sean and Jean come (/ kʌm /) home.

So she always does the work in a hurry ('hʌrɪ).

Yes, she does it with so much worry (/ 'wʌrɪ /).

She loves to wear gloves (glʌvz)

when she does the housework.

| [ o, u, ou ] | / ʌ / | cut | 56 |

Jean loves to keep a monkey and a dove.

She is saving all her pocket money (/ 'mʌnI /)

hoping to save enough (I'nʌf) to buy a puppy, too.

She knows it is really quite tough

to save enough money

to buy a monkey, a dove and a puppy.

She needs a lot of c<u>ou</u>rage (/ 'kʌrIdʒ /), too

to ask her mum to double her income

so that she can keep some pets for fun.

She knows it is rough to ask.

Jean's mum thinks she might be in trouble ('trʌbl)

if Jean sloughs off her pets after some time.

## 12. Vowel Phoneme / u: /

| Letter | Phoneme | Work | |
|--------|---------|------|------|
| [ oo ] | / u: / | moon | 57 |

Hed is only eight but he is so fat.

His face, well, is as round as the moon (/ mu:n /).

But he still wants so much food (/ fu:d /).

He thinks food keeps him in a good mood.

Hed's mum, Ned wants him to exercise with a hoop.

He thinks it fun to loop himself in the hoop.

Hed likes to loop in the hoop near the coop (/ ku:p /).

| [ oo ] | / u: / | moon | 58 |
|--------|--------|------|-----|

Hed's mum always laments as she says,

"Son, you are doomed to trouble soon (/ su:n /)

if you don't exercise after eating so much food."

She wants Hed to sweep all the rooms

with a big broom (/ bru:m /).

Hed likes to groom himself

in loose clothes and in boots

when he sweeps the rooms

Then he can have a little bit more food at noon (nu:n).

| [ oo, ou ] | / u: / | moon | 59 |

Hed has a pet goose called Luss  /  lu:s  / .

It is, well, so fat like Hed.

Hed always feeds Luss,

his pet goose with so much food.

He gives it a lot of roots in soup.

He even feeds it with a spoon.

Hed always thinks Luss,

his pet goose his boon companion.

| [ oo, ou, u ] | / u: / | moon | 60 |
|---|---|---|---|

Hed always lets Luss,

his pet goose go loose like a moose. (/ mu:s /)

Luss, Hed's pet goose likes

to go to the pool to keep cool.

Luss, Hed's pet goose always tries

to swim like a swan in the pool.

Hed thinks Luss looks like a fool

to swim like a swan.

But he thinks Luss is just cool

though it seems a bit crude (/ kru:d /).

| [ oo, ou, u ] | / u: / | moon | 61 |

Hed likes to go to the zoo.

There are geese in the zoo.

They are, well, as fat

as his pet goose, Luss.

He likes to look at the moose

and doodles under a cool shady tree

when he is in a good mood.

He is mooted to draw the moose near the pool

under the clear blue (blu:) sky.

| [ oo, ou, u ] | / u: / | moon | 62 |
|---|---|---|---|

Hed likes to watch a troop (tru:p) of monkeys

swinging in the trees higher than the roof.

Hed wishes to prove (pru:v)

that he can swing as high.

However, he finds it hard

to give a concrete proof (pru:f)

to swing in the tree

higher than the roof (ru:f).

| [ oo, ou, u ] | / u: / | moon | 63 |

Hed has a coupon for a group of three

to eat loon in soup (/ su:p /).

He likes to eat a lot.

But he thinks it cruel to eat loon

as it reminds him of his pet goose, Luss.

He would rather take nougat

and some vegetable soup.

| [ oo, ou, u ] | / uː / | moon | 64 |

The other day, the wind blew (/ bluː /) really hard.

Tutu, the fisherman quickly drew in his fishing net.

His crews Dudu and Fufu acted really fast

to bring in trays of cashew ('kæʃuː) nuts.

Dudu then went to brew some tea

to go with cashew nuts and cheese.

Tutu, Dudu and Fufu all liked to chew cashew nuts

when the wind blew really hard.

| [ oo, ou, u ] | / u: / | moon | 65 |

Tutu's wife, Nuru grew up on a farm.

She is very shrewd. (/ ʃruːd /)

She is a very good cook.

She knows how to cook

different kinds of food.

She often cooks stewed duck

with some cashew nuts.

She has a lot of knowledge, too.

She can tell you a mouse

from a shrew very well.

She knows the clues to tell the two (/ tuː /).

## 13. Vowel Phoneme / ʊ /

| Letter | Phoneme | Helping Word | |
|--------|---------|--------------|----|
| [ oo ] | / ʊ / | good | 66 |

Nuru has a very good (/ gʊ d /) cook (kʊk) book.

She always puts (pʊ ts) it in a drawer.

Yesterday, she took (tʊk) a look (lʊk) of the book (/ bʊk /).

She wanted to make some pudding (/ ˈpʊdɪŋ /)

for his son, Luke.

But Luke pushed (pʊʃt) and pulled (/ pʊ ld /) her

to sit down on the cushion (ˈk ʊʃən).

He wanted her to tell him

the story about a woman (/ ˈwʊmən /)

who kept a wolf (wʊlf) as her bosom (/ ˈbʊzəm /) friend.

| [ o, u ] | / ʊ / | book | 67 |
|---|---|---|---|

Tutu, Luke's dad keeps a bull called Duk  / dʊk /

and a rook called Guk  / gʊk / .

Duk, the bull is full of strength.

He can pull and push a load

many times his weight.

He can fulfil all the tasks

Tutu asks him to do.

But he cannot do much

when Guk, the rook hooks on his back.

| [ oo, u ] | / ʊ / | book | 68 |
|---|---|---|---|

Guk, the rook is not good (/ gʊd /).

She is a bully.

She likes to bully Duk, the bull.

She always hooks on Duk, the bull's back

and makes the sounds, "Luk! Luk!.............." / lʊk /

Duk, the bull wishes

he could push her off his back

and pull her around like a piece of wood (/ wʊd /).

and put her in a bag of wool (/ wʊl /).

## 14. Vowel Phonemes in comparison / u: / ʊ /, / ɒ / ɔ: / and / ɑ: / ʌ /

| | / u: / | / ʊ / | 69 |
|---|---|---|---|
| 1. | boot, root | foot, soot | |
| 2. | food | good, wood | |
| 3. | fool | wool | |
| 4. | proof, roof | poof | |

| | / ɒ / | / ɔ: / |
|---|---|---|
| 1. | bog | ball |
| 2. | cock | call |
| 3. | dog | door |
| 4. | fog | fall |
| 5. | hot | hall |

| | / ɑ: / | / ʌ / |
|---|---|---|
| 1. | barn | bun |
| 2. | calm | come |
| 3. | dart | dust |
| 4. | harsh | hush |
| 5. | mast | must |
| 6. | mask | musk |
| 7. | march | much |
| 8. | charm | chum |
| 9. | are | us |
| 10. | balm | bum |

## 15. Vowel Phoneme / əʊ /

| Letter | Phoneme | Word | |
|--------|---------|------|---|
| [ o ] | / əʊ / | O | 70-- 77 |

Sean has a friend called Ozee.

She likes to wear loose clothes at home (/ həʊm /).

She combs (k əʊ mz) her hair many times a day.

Ozee likes to go to the grocery (/ ˈgrəʊsərɪ /)

with her mum's, Olly.

Mr Ho, the grocer is always busy

talking on his mobile (ˈməʊ baɪl) phone (/ fəʊn /).

He always wears a big cross (/ kr əʊ s /)

across his big chest.

Ozee notices that he has fat big toes (təʊz)

twelve in number.

He always has a strong smell of lotion (ˈl əʊ ʃən).

His big fat toes always reminds her of the story

about a farmer who always carried a hoe.

He had a pet doe.

But he also had a foe.

| [ o ] | / əʊ / | O | 71 |
|-------|--------|---|-----|

Olly, Ozee's mum always says

Mr Ho is good and friendly.

He always opens his grocery store at 7am in the morning.

He only closes it at 7pm in the evening.

Then he goes home for motion pictures

to motivate (/ ˈməʊtɪveɪt /) himself.

You can buy almost everything

from lotus (/ ˈləʊtəs /) to toilet rolls from his store.

You can even call him toll-free.

But they never like to go to the store

next to the motor (/ məʊtə(r) /) lodge (lɒdʒ).

Mr Oh, the grocer, has a poker face.

He looks like a man full of motives.

| [ o-e, ow ] | / əʊ / | O | 72 |
| --- | --- | --- | --- |

Ozee has a skipping rope (/ rəʊp /).

She skips the rope every day.

She hopes she can skip

as well as her sister, Oyee.

Oyee can always cope

so well with her lessons

or in games in scope (/ skəʊp /).

Oyee has a mole (/ məʊl /) on her right cheek.

Ozee has a dimple on her left cheek.

The two sisters are poles (/ pəʊlz /) apart.

But they know they have different roles (/ rəʊlz /) in life.

| [ oa ] | / əʊ / | O | 73 |

Loho, Ozee's father has a pet goat called Load.

He likes to eat oat meal.

He can eat so much

until he looks so bloated (/ ˈbləʊtɪd /).

Then he lies flat on his stomach

beside the boat quite near the road and the moat.

He would groan and moan in regret

for eating so much oat (/ əʊt /).

| [ oa ] | / əʊ / | O | 74 |
| --- | --- | --- | --- |

Load, the goat likes to roam along the coast.

He likes to meet his friend, a toad called Hoad.

Hoad, the toad (təʊd) often coaxes,

Load, the goat to go for a swim.

Load, the goat would like to swim very much

like Hoad, the toad.

But he remembers his friend, Roach, a foal.

Roach, the foal, wanted to swim

like the goose, Poach in the moat.

But he found it hard to stay afloat.

Soon he groaned, moaned and foamed.

He got drowned in the moat.

| [ ol ] | / əʊ / | O | 75 |

Once there was an old man.

He always looked so and so cold (/ kəʊld /).

He liked gold so much so (/ səʊ /)

that he sold almost everything

in exchange for gold.

He always told the stories about god (g ɒ d) and gold (gəʊld).

He always liked to hold

a piece of gold in his hand

when he went to bed.

He believed he could meet

the god of gold in his dream

when he held a piece of gold in his hand.

| [ o, ou ] | / əʊ / | O | 76 |
|---|---|---|---|

Douglas likes to knead dough for his mum, Dolly

Dolly is a baker.

She likes to cast the dough (/ dəʊ /)

in the moulds (məʊldz) of different shapes and sizes.

Douglas always likes the cake and biscuits

his mum, Dolly makes.

He thinks they touch (tʌtʃ) his soul (səʊl)

to see cakes and biscuits

in different moulds of shapes and sizes.

Dolly, Douglas's mum also keep

some poultry for fun and food.

Cooking, baking and feeding her poultry (/ ˈpəʊltrɪ /)

keep her fully occupied (/ ˈɒ kjʊpaɪd /) daily.

| [ o, ou. ow, ] | / əʊ / | O | 77 |

Ozee's father Loho grow crops in rows (/ rəʊz /).

He owns (/ əʊnz /) a really big farm.

He never throws any crops (kr əʊ ps) he grows away.

He always gives unwanted crops to the poultry.

He always gets a good gross income every month.

Many people owe (/ əʊ /) him money

when they buy his crops on credit.

When the wind blows, the crops bow low.

The cock with a yellow cockscomb crows really loudly.

Loho, Ozee's dad sits at the window (/ 'wɪndəʊ /).

He watches helplessly how the soil flows away

with rainwater in rows.

## 16. Vowel Phoneme / ɔː /

| Letter | Phoneme | Word | |
|---|---|---|---|
| [ al, ar, au, aw, oar, or ] | / ɔː / | awe | 78 -- 83 |

Ball, Ozee's grandpa is a warm, bald and tall man.

He drinks quite a lot of plain water (/ ˈwɔːtə /) every day.

Of course, he likes to drink tea or coffee more.

He likes to go to the civic hall in town

to meet all his old friends.

He always likes to call them

at dawn (/ dɔːn /) for the meeting.

Then they will go to the food stall in a mall

to eat vegetables raw.

They all like rojak

and they always order (/ ˈɔːdə /) a whole big bowl.

| [ a, al, all, ar ] | / ɔ: / | awe | 79 |

Ball, Ozee's grandpa likes to talk

about World (/ w3:ld /) War II.

He always talks about how he got injured

when he walked about in August (/ 'ɔ:gəst /)

during World War II to warn the villagers of the war.

He had a short stay in a small ward (/ wɔ:d /)

with so many injured soldiers.

He can always remember a man

he saw with a broad jaw (/ dʒɔ: /).

He groaned in pain on a board in a corner (/ 'k ɔ:nə(r) /).

His both hands looked so coarse.

His voice sounded really hoarse (/ hɔ:s /)

that always daunted and haunted him all the time.

| [ al, au, aw, or, oor ] | / ɔː / | awe | 80 |
|---|---|---|---|

One of Sean's uncle called Paul is a lawyer.

He studied law in Australia ten years ago.

He often gives talk on the topic related to laws (/ lɔːz /).

Sean thinks law is boring (/ 'bɔːrIŋ /).

He always feels bored

when Paul, his uncle talks about laws.

But he is really puzzled and always wonders ('wʌdəz)

why his audience laud and applaud (/ ə'pl ɔːd /) so much

when he talks (/ tɔːks /) about laws.

His wife, Pauline, his son, Lawrence

and his daughter, Audery laugh

and hoot all the time

Sean thinks maybe his English is too poor

to understand the laws Paul, his uncle talks about.

| [ al, aw ] | / ɔː / | awe | 81 |
|---|---|---|---|

Sean's mum Mdm Chan has a pet cat called Yoyo.

Mdm Chan really adores Yoyo, her pet cat.

Yoyo, Mdm Chan pet cat has really long sharp claws

and four fat, big paws.

She likes to eat fish raw.

She can eat a lot.

Mdm Chan always says,

"My pet cat is not fat nor thin."

Sean will always quips saying,

"Your pet cat is plump, mum."

She often crawls out of the house

to look for her friends, Aw, Kaw and Naw

She likes to go out at dawn.

She yawns (jɔːnz) all the way out

and then all the way home.

| [ al, au, or ] | / ɔ: / | awe | 82 |
|---|---|---|---|

Mdm Moh, Sean's aunt thinks that her son,

Pow should take part in some sports (/ spɔːts /).

She thinks he can play basketball.

She always says, "You are not tall nor short."

Nor, Pow's sister, always quips saying,

"He is in normal height."

Mdm Moh always thinks that Pow needs

some more exercise to grow taller.

She thinks horse (/ hɔːs /) riding

or swimming is good for him.

He also needs to learn some music to tone up.

He may learn some sort of string chord (/ kɔːd /)

or choral singing.

He should be more participative in household chores, too.

| [ all, aw, or ] | / ɔ: / | awe | 83 |
|---|---|---|---|

Pow must go for all subject tuition every afternoon

from Monday to Friday.

He needs English tuition for two evenings.

Bahasa Malaysia is also important (/ Im'pɔ:tənt /).

He needs Bahasa Malaysia tuition for 2 evenings, too.

The Chinese subject also needs some attention.

He may go for one evening.

He has drawing lessons every Saturday morning.

He has to go for horse riding

or swimming every Saturday afternoon.

He may go shopping with the family

on Saturday evenings.

On Sunday mornings, he must go

to church, mosque or temple

to learn some core (/ k ɔ: (r) /) values.

On Sunday afternoons, he may call

or play with his friends.

For Sunday evenings, yes, he may relax at home

with some board (/ bɔ:d /) games.

## 17. Vowel Phoneme / ɜː /

| Letter | Phoneme | Word | |
|---|---|---|---|
| [ ear, er, ir, ur ] | / ɜː / | early | 84 |

Once there was an earl (/ ɜːl /).

He always got up so early in the morning.

He needed to earn a living.

He was always so earnest to serve (/ sɜːv /) others.

He always dug everywhere

to look for some earthworms (/ ˈɜːθwɜːm /)

for his girlfriend's goldfish at home.

Everybody thought he was

the most earnest (/ ˈɜːnɪst /) earl on earth.

| [ er, ir ] | / ɜː / | early | 85 |

Birch is a very nervous (ˈnɜːvəs) person.

He is always on alert (əˈlɜːt).

He jerks easily

when he moves the herd of cow around.

He is certain he is safe

in the fern-filled, fertile land

with so many plants of herb.

He likes to perch on a really huge rock

to day-dream of the girl,

Yerp (jɜːp) he loves.

| [ er, ir, ur ] | / ɜː / | early | 86 |
|---|---|---|---|

Er-erh (/ ˈɜːɜːh /) is one of Sean's classmates.

She keeps her birds in a big cage.

She has a parrot first (fɜːt) and then a sparrow.

The bird of paradise is the third (θɜːd) bird she has.

Her birds always chirp so much.

They are always in much mirth all day long.

Herlang (ˈhɜːlɑŋ), Er-erh's mum is firm.

First, she wants to make sure that

her birds do not stir

and disturb their quiet neighbours.

| [ er, ir, ur ] | / ɜ: / | early | 87 |
|---|---|---|---|

Er-erh has a little brother called Jern-erh (/ ˈdʒɜːnɜːh /).

They have an aunt called Gerleh (/ ˈgɜːləh /),

who is a nurse.

She might go for further studies.

Jern-erh gurgles and berps a lot

when he turns on his stomach on the floor.

He is so scared of turkeys.

He is also allergy to fur

and some plastic furniture (/ ˈfɜːnItʃə /).

He likes his grandparents murmuring to him.

and he always gurgles and coos in response.

Herlang, Er-erh's mum always brings him

to church on Sundays.

He always wears a purple coat

and he gurgles and smiles a lot more.

## 18. Vowel Phoneme / ə /

| Letter | Phoneme | Word | |
|---|---|---|---|
| [ a, e, i, o, u [ ar, er, or, ure ] | / ə / | ago | 88 |

Once there was a beggar (/ 'begə(r) /)

who kept a lot of calendars (/ 'kæləndə(r) /).

He liked celery in his diet ('daɪət).

He always went to a charity ('tʃærətɪ) centre

for his meals and chattered ('tʃætəd).

But he never liked to stay (steɪ)

in the big chamber

with so many other members.

He preferred to move around (/ ə'raʊnd /)

carrying a big bag of calendars.

The vowel letters "a, e, o, or u" may have / ə / or / ɪ / speech sound in unstressed syllable(s).

| [ a, e, i, o, u er ] | / ə / | ago / əˈgəu / | 89 |

Sean's best friend is called Engel (/ ˈendʒəl /).

She loves her father (/ ˈfɑːðə(r) /), mother, brother (ˈbrʌðə(r))

and sister so much.

Her ambition (/ æmˈbɪʃən /) is to be a teacher (/ ˈtiːtʃə(r) /).

She is so clever (/ ˈklevə(r) /).

She never fools around.

She has an uncle who is a doctor (/ ˈdɒktə(r) /).

He is a part-time actor, too.

He has given her a thermometer in celsius (/ ˈselsɪəs /)

and with sensor.

Sometimes she plays a doctor

with her pet hamster.

They always have a lot of fun

and in good consensus.

She always thinks her pet hamster

her good companion (/ kəmˈpænɪən /)

| [ a, e, i, o, u er ] | / ə / | ago / ə'gəu / | 90 |
|---|---|---|---|

Chong-Sherh (/ 'tʃɒŋ ʃəh /) has a lot of brochures.

He likes to look at the pictures (/ 'pIktʃəs /)

on different subject matters.

He has kept a lot of travel brochures (/ 'brəuʃəs /).

He likes to observe the buildings

with different architectures ('a:kItektʃəs).

He thinks some brochures really provides him

with a lot of information about different cultures.

He always wears clothes in cotton(/ 'kɒtn /) textures (tekstʃəs).

He thinks he is likely to take up

the course of agriculture (/ 'ægrIkʌltʃə(r) /) as a career (/ kə'rIə(r) /).

## 19. Diphthong / aɪ /

| Letter | Phoneme | Word | |
|--------|---------|------|----|
| [ i ] | / aɪ / | I, ice | 91 |

Sean has a little neighbour called Irene.

She likes to eat apples and pineapples.

She is only five (faɪv) years old.

But she can ride a bicycle for aged nine.

She can climb up a tree really fast.

She is not scared of lice or mice.

She always says she is not scared of the tiger, either (/ aɪðə(r) /).

She always says that a tiger is a cat huge in size.

But she always has a fright

when Fu-I, (/ ˈfuːaɪ /) her little brother,

has a sudden scream behind her.

| [ i ] | / aɪ / | I | 92 |

Irene always thinks that

Sean is kind and nice.

He always lets her have a bite

of his ice-cream when he has one.

Irene really likes ice-cream.

But her mum only gives her some.

She has to eat a portion of fish,

some vegetables and rice

She has two dices that she likes so much.

She feels like to give one to Sean.

But her elder sister, I-an, (/ ˈaɪən /) advised her

to think twice or thrice.

The two dices are unique

and can fetch a price.

| [ i ] | / aɪ / | I | 93 |
|---|---|---|---|

Irene likes to go to the playground to climb (/ klaɪm /) and glide,

when the weather is fine.

The road to the playground is not wide.

But it has so many flowers on both sides.

She always likes to go there to play hide-and-seek.

She also can ride her bicycle.

Or she can just stride (/ straɪd /) around with Fu-I,

with their mother walking leisurely a little behind.

| [ i ] | / aɪ / | I | 94 |

One of Engel's uncle is a doctor called Mike Chai.

Nino (/ ˈnaɪnə /) is his wife.

She is a writer and she writes well.

She is friendly, kind and nice.

She always smiles to others readily and says, 'Hi'.

She always says, "Smiling does not cost you a dime.

Smile whenever you can, fine or not fine.

It, for sure, makes you look so divine."

She can walk a mile or two every day.

Then she needs to sit down for a while

and enjoy the drinks with lemon and lime.

| [ i ] | / aɪ / | I | 95 |

Dr. Mike Chai and his wife, Nino, have two children.

Ching Chai, their son is nine.

Mary Chai, their daughter is five.

Ching Chai really likes kite-flying.

But he seems never able to fly his kite

higher than a house or a tree.

Soon it gets entangled somewhere.

Mary Chai always sighs (/ saɪz /) at the sight beside him.

Ching Chai would shrug his shoulders

and try to smile and appear light.

Instead of fussing and fretting,

he watches other people

flying their kites so high into the sky.

Then, he would say, "One day, I will fly my kite

as high into the sky."

Nino, his mum, always nods and smiles.

| [ i ] | / aI / | I | 96 |
| --- | --- | --- | --- |

Dr. Mike Chai has a dog called Zai.

It has white fur and two really bright eyes.

Zai likes to roam about at night

behind the house.

When he feels threatened,

he always thinks for a while,

to fight or flight.

He always chooses to flight

He does not like to fight

as he might get hurt.

Then Dr. Mike Chai, his master,

might be tight on him.

He might be denied the right

to go out at night.

He does not want to be in such a plight.

| [ i ] | / aɪ / | I | 97 |
|-------|--------|---|-----|

Last year, Sean had a hamster called Wai-I (/ ˈwaɪaɪ /).

He loved Wai-I so much.

He never tied it up nor put it in a cage.

He let it go free to roam about.

He gave it ice-cream, pizza and pie (/ paɪ /).

Wai-I, the hamster really liked the food.

Sean always gave Wai-I

so much ice-cream, pizza and pie to eat

Wai-I always enjoyed the food to the bursting full.

One day, Sean saw Wai-I lying motionless

with a big stomach full of ice-cream, pizza and pie

Sean realised that Wai-I had died

with too much ice-cream, pizza and pie.

For the loss, he cried and cried day and night.

## 20. Diphthong / aʊ /

| Letter clusters | Phoneme | Helping words | |
|---|---|---|---|
| [ ou, ow ] | / aʊ / | loud, cow | 98 -- |

Oyee, Ozee's sister, has a pet owl called Howhow ('haʊhəʊ).

Howhow has brown feathers and two big round eyes.

She likes to perch on the branch of a tree

to look at the crowd.

She only comes down to the ground for a while

when Oyee is around.

Ozee always thinks Oyee's pet owl (/ aʊl /),

Howhow as stiff as a king

with a big crown on his head in a story.

| [ ou, ow ] | / aʊ / | cow | 99 |
|---|---|---|---|

Ozee's younger brother, Oho has

a pet mouse called How-our (/ ˈhaʊaʊ /).

How-our is very scared of

Loho's pet hound (/ h aʊ nd /) called Pound.

He always shivers

when he hears Pound, the hound, howls.

How-our always stays in the house

when Pound, the hound is around.

He does not even dare to stay

in the mouse-hole

in a mound outside the house.

He would only go to see his friend, Dowl (/ daʊl /), a fowl

when Pound, the hound is not around.

| [ ou, ow ] | / aʊ / | how | 100 |
|---|---|---|---|

Wow-mow ('waʊməʊ) is a clown.

He always wears a blouse and a gown.

He likes to powder himself all over.

Then he wipes himself with a towel ('taʊəl).

He keeps many fowls

and counts them every day.

Last Sunday, he found some of the hen fowls

started laying eggs.

The hen fowls seem to make

a lot of sounds nowadays.

He often sees eggs around

on the ground in the compound.

| [ ou, ow ] | / aʊ / | now | 101 |
| --- | --- | --- | --- |

Wow-mow, the clown always thinks

the tower near his house has some magic power.

He always thinks the tower

has the power to revitalise him.

He likes to climb up to the top of the tower (/ ˈtaʊə(r) /)

to look at the clouds and shout out loud.

He likes to say,

"I am proud of myself being a happy clown."

## 21. Diphthong / ɔɪ /

| Letter clusters | Phoneme | Helping words | |
|---|---|---|---|
| [ oi, oy ] | / ɔɪ / | oil, boy | 102 – 105 |

Sean has a cousin called Joy.

He is a two-year old boy.

But he is not so jovial.

He always makes so much noise (nɔɪz).

He wants his mum to be around all the time.

He wants to play with his friend, Doy (/ dɔɪ /)

When his mum is around,

you can hardly hear his voice (vɔɪs).

He enjoys his mum's company (/ 'kʌmpənɪ /).

When he plays with his friend, Doy and Moy,

he is no more fussy nor noisy.

| [ oi, oy ] | / ɔɪ / | boy | 103 |

Sean has an uncle called Roy.

For breakfast, he likes to eat

a boiled egg and a coiled (/ kɔɪld /) bun.

He prefers broiled chicken

or some beef for lunch.

For dinner, he eats only rice, fruit, beans

and some vegetables cooked with little oil.

He takes some cereal for snack, too.

He would like some noodles

if he has a choice (/ tʃɔɪs /).

| [ oi, oy ] | / ɔɪ / | boy | 104 |
|---|---|---|---|

Roy leads a cloistered life.

He avoids (/ əˈvɔɪdz /) people

if he has a choice.

He joins only Nature Society

to keep himself buoyant (/ ˈbɔɪənt /)

He tilts soil to grow crops

he toils hard to earn a living

so that he can enjoy his life.

His joints ache sometimes

and he always groans and moans "Aioy! Aioy!"

He always applies some ointment

to keep his skin moist.

He has a pet dog called Royal (/ ˈrɔɪəl /).

Roy keeps coins and doilies as hobbies.

This is the little foible (/ ˈfɔɪbl /)

that Choi, his loyal (/ ˈl ɔɪ əl /) wife sees he has.

Choi, his loyal wife always helps him

to look around for more.

| [ oi, oy ] | / ɔɪ / | boy | 105 |

Roy always keeps the toilets sparklingly clean.

He wants the toilets to look really spick and span.

So he cleans the toilets many times a day.

He only cleans them with water

or garbage enzyme and a brush

He always thinks toilet detergent too poisonous. (/ ˈpɔɪzənəs /)

He never points at his loyal wife, Choi

and find-fault for not keeping the house as clean

He never reprimands his pet dog, Royal for the mess.

He is no doubt a man of great poise.

He knows, "One man's food is another man's poison." (/ ˈpɔɪzən /)

## 22. Diphthong / Iə /

| Letter clusters | Phoneme | Helping Words | 106 – 109 |
|---|---|---|---|

| | | |
|---|---|---|
| [ ear, eer, ere, ] | / Iə / | ear, deer, here |
| [ ier, eir, ia, ion ] | | fierce, weird, aria, onion |

Pound, the hound is fully geared for hunting.

He has two sharp ears (/ Iəz /) to hear (/ hIə /) so well.

He has two bright big eyes to see

animals or insects as well.

He has a very sensitive big nose to smell

or discern anything not so near (/ nIə(r) /).

He has the teeth as sharp as the spear.

He has the claws to tear (/ teə(r) /) and pierce (/ pIəs /).

How-our always shivers in fear

when he hears Pound, the hound

pow-bow and howl so loud.

| [ ear, eer, ere, eir ] | / Iə / | ear | 107 |
|---|---|---|---|

Loho's pet deer, Sphere (/ sfIə /) never likes Pound, the hound.

Sphere, the deer, always thinks Pound, the hound

looks really fierce and weird (/ wIəd /).

His two ears always look so pricked up and stiff.

His nose seems to flick so much to scent.

He even bares his teeth without a cause.

He spreads out his claws every now and then.

He is just queer (/ kwIə(r) /).

He likes to walk here and there.

He even sneers at a mere (/ mIə (r) /) housefly.

| [ ear, eer, eir, ere ] | / Iə / | ear | 108 |
|---|---|---|---|

Sphere, the deer, does not like

Pound, the hound to get near him.

He thinks Pound, the hound

has a really strong smell of onion (/ ˈʌnIən /).

It looks like he is infested

by bacteria (/ bækˈtIərIə /) in millions or billions.

When Loho rides his motorbike, Pound, the hound

likes to take a pillion (/ ˈpIlIən /) seat for a ride.

At times, he likes to rear up

on his hind legs to please Loho, his master.

| [ ear, eer, eir, ere ] | / Iə / | ear | 109 |

How-our, the mouse is always so timid.

He is scared of Pound, the hound.

He is scared of the shears (/ ʃIəz /)

that Loho, the farmer carries here and there.

He gets easily in tears

whenever he sees the shears.

He knows he has to be careful

when he scampers past the fireplace.

He is scared of getting seared. (sIəd)

Of course, he has to be cautious

not to smear the place.

He may cheer and steer (/ stIə /) Oho's toy car about

when nobody is around.

## 23. Diphthong / eə /

| Letter clusters | Phoneme | Helping Words | |
|---|---|---|---|
| [ ear, air ] | / eə / | bear, air, ware | |
| [ are, eir ] | | heir | 110 – 112 |

Ozee has a teddy bear (/ beə(r) /).

She likes to sit it on a chair.

She likes to wear a pink T-shirt

and a blue skirt.

Sometimes she ties up her hair

in a ponytail.

Sometimes she pins her hair up.

She wants to look really fair (/ feə(r) /),

so she eats a pear every day.

| [ are, ear, air, eir | / eə / | air | 111 |
| --- | --- | --- | --- |

Ozee swears she has the flair (/ fleə(r) /)

to become a good athlete (/ ˈæθliːt /).

She can walk up and down the stairs really fast.

For sure, there is no tear (/ teə(r) /) or wear of her shoes.

But she would not dare to take part

in 100 or 200 metre race

She knows she cannot run as fast as Pearl (/ pɜːl /).

Pearl can run as fast as a hare (heə(r)).

She practises running every day.

But Ozee does not want to spare

even an afternoon or two for running practice

to become a good athlete.

| [ are, ear, air, eir ] | / eə / | air | 112 |
|---|---|---|---|

Ozee is aware (/ ə'weə(r) /) that she is a little bit fat.

Olly, Ozee's mum, always says,

"You should take care of your weight."

Ozee does not dare to blare

that she can one day run like a hare.

Ozee thinks she should go to the square (/ skweə(r) /)

for more exercise to fare well in life.

When Oho teases her to be like a piggy in clothes,

she glares and snarl (/ snɑ:l /) at him like a lion

with bushy mare.

She really flares up in anger.

Oho is scared and stares at her

and gets prepared (/ prɪ'peə(r)d /) to fight or flight.

Olly, their mum would have to put aside

the cookware and be on alert and aware

that they might be a fight.

## 24. Diphthong / ʊə /

| Letter clusters | Phoneme | Helping Words | 113 |
|---|---|---|---|

| | | | |
|---|---|---|---|
| [ oor, our ] | / ʊə / | boor, tour | |
| [ ur, ua ] | | lure, actual | |

Roy has a bother called Royce.

Royce is a gourmet. (/ ˈgʊəmeɪ /)

He is a gourmand (/ ˈgʊəmənd /), too.

But he never likes the food

made from gourd of any kind.

He is always lured to food.

He always tours

or detours around for food.

Royce's wife, Joyce, is a pianist.

She plays the piano well.

She has to think hard and fast

what alluring dishes to cook.

Very often Royce chooses

to cook the foods of his choice.

Royce likes to write books, too,

describing the luscious (/ ˈlʌʃəs /) foods.

## 25. Diphthongs in comparison

| / əʊ / | / aʊ / | 114 |
|--------|--------|-----|
| low, blow | cow, how, now, owl | |
| bow | bow | |
| row, grow, crow | crowd | |
| own | down, town, gown, | |
| | clown, crown, brown, | |

| / ɪə / | / ɜː / | / eə / |
|--------|--------|--------|
| tear | earl | tear |
| spear | pearl | pear |
| ear | | bear |
| fear, hear, gear, | | wear, swear |
| near, rear, sear, | | |
| smear, shear, | | |
| here, mere, sphere | | there, where |

| / ɑː / | / eə / |
|--------|--------|
| are | bare, blare, care, dare, flare, glare, |
| | hare, mare, spare, share, snare, square, |
| | stare, ware |

## 26. Consonant Phonemes

| No. | Phonemes | Helping Words | |
|-----|----------|---------------|---|
| 1. | / p / | p --- pen | 115 |
| 2. | / b / | b --- bed | |

| No. | Phonemes | Helping Words |
|-----|----------|---------------|
| 3. | / t / | t --- tea |
| 4. | / d / | d --- desk |

| No. | Phonemes | Helping Words |
|-----|----------|---------------|
| 5. | / k / | c --- uncle / k ---ankle / ch --- mechanic |
| 6. | / g / | g --- girl |

| No. | Phonemes | Helping Words |
|-----|----------|---------------|
| 7. | / ʃ / | sh -- she / t -- patient / c -- ocean |
| 8. | / ʒ / | s -- leisure |

| No. | Phonemes | Helping Words |
|-----|----------|---------------|
| 9. | / tʃ / | ch – chair |
| 10. | / dʒ / | ge – orange / dge – bridge / J -- June |

| No. | Phonemes | Helping Words |
|-----|----------|---------------|
| 11. | / f / | f – fly / gh – rough / ph – elephant |
| 12. | / v / | v – vase |

| No. | Phonemes | Helping Words |
|-----|----------|---------------|
| 13. | / s / | s – sea / c – cell / x – box |
| 14. | / z / | z – zoo / s – boys / es – houses |

| | | | |
|---|---|---|---|
| 15. | / θ / | th – three | 116 |
| 16. | / ð / | th – father | |

| | | |
|---|---|---|
| 17. | / h / | h -- hat |

| | | |
|---|---|---|
| 18. | / m / | m – mother |
| 19. | / n / | n – no / n – on |
| 20. | / ŋ / | nk – sink / ng – sing |

| | | |
|---|---|---|
| 21. | / l / | l – all / l -- like |
| 22. | / r / | r -- red |
| 23. | / j / | y – yes |
| 24. | / w / | w – we |

Sean is going to a camp.

He needs to bring along a few things.

He needs a pen to write or describe.

He needs a pan to fly an egg or two.

He needs to carry along a sleeping bag

and a backpack.

He needs some clothes pegs, too.

He also needs to bring three or four apples.

He wants to eat an apple a day

so that he is able to keep the doctor away.

| Consonant pair | [ p b ] | / p b / | 118 |

Jet, Dr. Vet's pet dog likes to go to the park so much.

He barks furiously when it is time to go to the park.

But when he hears Mdm Chan batter in the kitchen

and Dr. Vet patter on the phone,

Jet will bark out loud to remind them

that he wants to go to the park.

However, if he is not attended to.

His bark would turn into a howl.

He would pow-bow ('paʊbaʊ) all the time.

He behaves more like a pest than a pet.

Dr. Vet thinks it not the best dog he has kept.

Mdm Chan bets Dr. Vet would like to beat it in the peat.

| Consonant pair | [ p b ] | / p b / | 119 |

The weather is bad.

Sean feels cold and bored.

So, he stays in bed to draw, read or dream.

He has drawn a big pig

beside a small bin

and some safety pins.

He is reading a book about a big pig.

The big pig has a small bin

and some safety pins.

When the big pig is taking a nap,

a bat always flies in the sty to pat him.

He almost nabs the bat in the act.

|     | / p /  |            | / b /   |                 |
| --- | ------ | ---------- | ------- | --------------- |
| 1.  | pat    | / pæt /    | bat     | / bæt /         |
| 2.  | pet    | / pet /    | bet     | / bet /         |
| 3.  | pest   | / pest /   | best    | / best /        |
| 4.  | pent   | / pent /   | bent    | / bent /        |
| 5.  | pig    | / pɪg /    | big     | / bɪg /         |
| 6.  | pin    | / pɪn /    | bin     | / bɪn /         |
| 7.  | pit    | / pɪt /    | bit     | / bɪt /         |
| 8.  | nap    | / næp /    | nab     | / næb /         |
| 9.  | * pass | / pɑːs /   | bass    | / beɪs / , / bæs / |
| 10. | peat   | / piːt /   | beat    | / biːt /        |
| 11. | pay    | / peɪ /    | bay     | / beɪ /         |
| 12. | park   | / pɑːk /   | bark    | / bɑːk /        |
| 13. | patter | / ˈpætə(r) / | batter | / ˈbætə(r) /   |
| 14. | plank  | / plæŋk /  | blank   | / blæŋk /       |
| 15. | pray   | / preɪ /   | bray    | / breɪ /        |
| 16. | lap    | / læp /    | lab     | / læb /         |
| 17. | tap    | / tæp /    | tab     | / tæb /         |
| 18. | rip    | / rɪp /    | rib     | / rɪb /         |
| 19. | sip    | / sɪp /    | sib     | / sɪb /         |
| 20. | mop    | / mɒp /    | mob     | / mɒb /         |
| 21. | sop    | / sɒp /    | sob     | / sɒb /         |
| 22. | pack   | / pæk /    | back    | / bæk /         |
| 23. | pan    | / pæn /    | ban     | / bæn /         |

Minimal pairs are pairs of words which are marked by the difference of a speech sound / phoneme, for example, "pat / pæt / and bat / bæt /". For the pair "pass / pɑːs / and bass / beɪs / " are not considered as a minimal pair because there are more than one differences in speech sounds.

Once there were ten tigers

living in a den.

They are always making awful din

with the tins.

They liked to hit the metal wares

with the medals.

There were many things they like

to do together in unison.

They felt sad if they sat

in the den doing nothing.

They liked to make a long trip

until they dripped so much.

Then they got the tips to go

somewhere for a dip.

They liked to play the game, hit-and-hide.

They really thought the game,

tie-and-die, really fun.

The ten tigers really had a good time

there and then.

| Consonant pair | [ t d ] | / t d / | 122 |

Once there was a woman called Tidy.

She always pedalled around

to sell flowers with petals.

She easily moved to tears

when she saw her children dear

good and obedient.

She always pedalled hard to go downtown

to sell flowers with petals.

To ride her old bicycle around

to sell flowers was like a rite in life

she had to perform daily.

Sometimes when wild dogs chased her,

she would beat them with her string of beads

if she needed.

| Consonant pair | [ t d ] | / t d / | 123 |

Tidy always told her children stories

when she was free.

The children liked to listen to the story

about an old man.

He wanted to wear his only tie

when he was about to die.

They liked the story

about an old woman, too.

She always cooked food

in a pot without a lid.

But when she thought

the pot needed a lid

to cook well.

She lit the candle to look for it.

|      |        | / t /       |         | / d /       |
|------|--------|-------------|---------|-------------|
| 1.   | ten    | / ten /     | den     | / den /     |
| 2.   | tear   | / tɪə(r) /  | dear    | / dɪə(r) /  |
| 3.   | tie    | / taɪ /     | die     | / daɪ /     |
| 4.   | tin    | / tɪn /     | din     | / dɪn /     |
| 5.   | tip    | / tɪp /     | dip     | / dɪp /     |
| 6.   | trip   | / trɪp /    | drip    | / drɪp /    |
| 7.   | to     | / tu: /     | do      | / du: /     |
| 8.   | *ton   | / tʌn /     | *don    | / dɒn /     |
| 9.   | tub    | / tʌb /     | dub     | / dʌb /     |
| 10.  | tune   | / tju:n /   | dune    | / dju:n /   |
| 11.  | metal  | / 'metl /   | medal   | / 'medl /   |
| 12.  | mettle | / 'metl /   | meddle  | / 'medl /   |
| 13.  | petal  | / 'petl /   | pedal   | / 'pedl /   |
| 14.  | bit    | / bɪt /     | bid     | / bɪd /     |
| 15.  | hit    | / hɪt /     | hid     | / hɪd /     |
| 16.  | kit    | / kɪt /     | kid     | / kɪd /     |
| 17.  | rite   | / raɪt /    | ride    | / raɪd /    |
| 18.  | mat    | / mæt /     | mad     | / mæd /     |
| 19.  | pat    | / pæt /     | pad     | / pæd /     |
| 20.  | sat    | / sæt /     | sad     | / sæd /     |
| 21.  | hat    | / hæt /     | had     | / hæd /     |
| 22.  | fat    | / fæt /     | fad     | / fæd /     |

| 23. | lat | / læt / | lad | / læd / | 125 |
|-----|------|---------|-------|----------|-----|
| 24. | treat | / triːt / | tread | / tred / | |
| 25. | neat | / niːt / | knead | / niːd / | |
| 26. | wet | / wet / | wed | / wed / | |
| 27. | met | / met / | med | / med / | |
| 28. | trill | / trɪl / | drill | / drɪl / | |
| 29. | peat | / piːt / | bead | / biːd / | |
| 30. | tank | / tæŋk / | dank | / dæŋk / | |
| 31. | lit | / lɪt / | lid | / lɪd / | |
| 32. | town | / taʊn / | down | / daʊn / | |

Joy has a big sister called Kigi.

Kigi is a seven-year-old girl.

Her hair is curly and always entangled.

She entangles her hair even more

when she combs her hair.

She wears an anklet around her left leg.

She always throws her toy anchor in anger.

She always wants her toy goat to wear a coat.

She likes to kick and dig around.

Joy never likes his sister Kigi.

He thinks she is spoilt rotten

when she throws her toy anchor in anger.

| Consonant pair | [ k g ] | / k g / | 127 |

Kugi enjoys helping his parents on the farm.

When he is tired,

he always sags on the sacks in the shed.

He likes to wear a cap with a gap.

Yesterday he really dug

so many earthworms for the ducks.

Today he wants to pick some beans

and nuts for the pigs.

He always grows some crops for his pet crow.

He never likes to lock his pet dog in a cage.

The dog always likes to roam about even to the dock.

| Consonant pair | [ k g ] | / k g / | 128 |
| --- | --- | --- | --- |

Kugi has friend called Guku.

He came yesterday for a game.

Today he has come with chewing gum.

He reads a lot.

He likes to tell stories.

He told Kugi a story

about a fish with big gills that could kill.

Kugi likes the story about a brave goat.

The goat gored the monster to death

when it cored the fruits in the orchard.

Kugi thinks the story

about how the cones of the ice-cream

had gone is very interesting, too.

Guku suddenly changes the tack

and wants to play a game called tag.

| | / k / | | / g / | |
|---|---|---|---|---|
| 1. | came | / keɪm / | game | / geɪm / |
| 2. | cap | / kæp / | gap | / gæp / |
| 3. | coat | / kəʊt / | goat | / gəʊt / |
| 4. | come | / kʌm / | gum | / gʌm / |
| 5. | cone | * / kəʊn / | gone | * / gɒn / |
| 6. | core | / kɔ:(r) / | gore | / gɔ:(r) / |
| 7. | crow | / krəʊ / | grow | / grəʊ / |
| 8. | curl | / kɜ:l / | girl | / gɜ:l / |
| 9. | duck | / dʌk / | dug | / dʌg / |
| 10. | dock | / dɒk / | dog | / dɒg / |
| 11. | kill | / kɪl / | gill | / gɪl / |
| 12. | anchor | / 'æŋkə(r) / | anger | / 'æŋgə(r) / |
| 13. | ankle | / 'æŋkl / | angle | / 'æŋgl / |
| 14. | lack | / læk / | lag | / læg / |
| 15. | lock | / lɒk / | log | / lɒg / |
| 16. | pick | / pɪk / | pig | / pɪg / |
| 17. | pluck | / plʌk / | plug | / plʌg / |
| 18. | sack | / sæk / | sag | / sæg / |
| 19. | tack | / tæk / | tag | / tæg / |
| 20. | track | / træk / | drag | / dræg / |

Oyee is too shy to take part

in a speech competition (/ ˌkɒmpə'tɪʃn /).

She feels that she is under great pressure (/ 'preʃə(r) /).

Olly, her mum says she should take it

as a kind of pleasure (/ 'pleʒə(r) /).

She should see it as a good measure

to her progress ('prəʊgrəs).

She should treasure (/ 'treʒə(r) /)

this golden opportunity to develop (/ dɪ'veləp /) herself.

She could practise it at leisure.

But she should pay some attention

to stress, pronunciation, and intonation.

She should be patient with herself

and she can make it.

| Consonant pair | [ sh, s ] | / ʃ ʒ / | 131 |

How-our, the mouse likes to sneak out of the house

to meet his friend, Dow, the fowl in the bushes.

He scampers to the bushes (/ 'bʊʃəz /)

when Pound, the hound is not around.

He always brings some bread crumbs, rice

and orange cake pieces to share with pleasure.

Dow, the fowl, has nuts, seeds and grains to share, too.

Occasionally (/ ə'keɪʒnəlɪ /), they will go to the river

teeming with fish to wash (/ wɒʃ /) their feet

and have spa at leisure (/ 'leʒə(r) /).

They always have a lot of fun.

| Consonant pair | [ s, sh, t ] | / ʃ ʒ / | 132 |

Pound, the hound always thinks How-our so weird.

He seems to dash and rush (/ rʌʃ /)

here and there for nothing.

He seems to be in great tension (/ ˈtenʃn /).

He loses all his composure (/ kəmˈpəʊʒə(r) /)

when Pound, the hound meets him just in case.

Pound, the hound always gives others

the negative impression.

How-our always thinks Pound, the hound

only possesses the hunting quotient (/ ˈkwəʊʃnt /).

How-our once saw Pound, the hound pin

Croak, the frog under his fat big paw and said, "Hello!"

He caused so much shame (/ ʃeɪm /)

to Croak, the frog without knowing it.

Ruich (ruːItʃ), Page's mum knows

how to make jelly very well.

Page likes to watch her making jelly ('dʒelI)

and wishes he could make for himself one day.

Ruich, his mum teaches (/ 'tiːtʃəz /) Page each (/ iːtʃ /) time

how to make milk jelly.

But he just cannot make the jelly

have the taste he wishes.

Page's ambition is to become a chef (/ ʃef /) one day.

Ruich, Page's mum makes jam (dʒæm), too

and puts it in a jar (/ dʒɑː (r) /).

She grinds fruit juice (/ dʒuːs /)

three times a week for the family.

She gives each a glass of juice to enjoy (/ In'dʒɔI /).

She makes sandwiches ('sænwItʃəz) every other days.

Page always quips saying, "We do not need to go

to the beach to eat sandwich." (/ 'sænwItʃ /)

Page (/ peIdʒ /) wishes he could have jam, jelly, sandwiches

and fruit juice every day.

Ruich, his mum, tries to teach him to make each kind

when she has a chance (/ tʃɑːns /).

She always says it is good for a boy

to be a real chef full-time or part-time.

| Consonant pair | [ ch, ge ] | / tʃ dʒ / | 134 |

Skitch, Page's dad is really rich.

He keeps badges (/ ˈbædʒəz /) as a hobby.

He always wears a badge.

He likes to bring his family to the beach (/ biːtʃ /).

He enjoys sandwiches (/ sænwɪtʃəz /)

and orange juice for lunch.

Skitch, Page's dad has kept an ostrich called Twitch.

He never keeps Twitch, the ostrich in a cage.

Twitch, the ostrich is always free

to move about within the compound.

Skitch always says,

"You need to have rich knowledge (/ ˈnɒlɪdʒ /)

to keep an ostrich."

Skitch, Page's dad tries hard to teach

Twitch, the ostrich some rules and regulations

of a domestic pet.

| Consonant pair | [ ch, j, ge, t ] | / tʃ dʒ / | 135 |

Page wishes he had a chance to go camping.

He thinks crossing the overhanging bridge is exciting.

Pitching the tent at the edge (/ edʒ /)

of the forest is fun, too.

Richard (/ ˈrɪtʃəd /), his good friend, would like to adventure, for sure.

He and Richard believe there are witches

living in caves somewhere in the forest.

They can switch from one form to another easily.

They can fly about freely.

Page thinks it such an adventure (/ ədˈventʃə(r) /) to reach there.

He often imagines (/ ɪˈmædʒɪn /) of meeting the Seven Dwarfs

like Snow White.

He has the itch to wear like a witch to roam about.

He likes to play the juggler (/ ˈdʒʌglə(r) /) at times.

He is such an imaginative (ɪˈmædʒɪnətɪv) boy.

| / ʃ / | / ʒ / |
|---|---|
| 1. pressure | pleasure, measure, treasure |
| 2. sure | leisure, composure, closure |
| 3. discussion, mission | allusion, cohesion, occasion, |
| pension, tension | vision, television |
| 4. luxury | luxuriant, luxurious |
| 5. assure | azure |

Consonants in Comparison     / tʃ dʒ /

| / tʃ / | / tʃ -- dʒ / | / dʒ / |
|---|---|---|
| 1. char | | jar |
| 2. ranch | | range |
| 3. rich | | ridge |
| 4. chug | | jug |
| 5. choose | | juice |
| 6. chunk | | junk |
| 7. *church | | judge |
| 8. chump | | jump |
| 9. chop | | jog |
| 10. | change | |
| 11. | charge | |

Engel has a toy fan.

She has a toy van, too.

She feels very happy

when she takes a ride of a ferry.

She likes to see the vast view

of the sky joining the sea.

There are always a few

seagulls flying freely around.

She thinks taking a ferry ride is fun

as the ferry never goes too fast.

She feels safe in a ferry.

This saves her from fear and worry.

| Consonant pair | [ gh ] | / f v / | 138 |
|---|---|---|---|

Roy's pet dog, Royal is tough (/ tʌf /).

But he can be very rough (/ rʌf /).

He never thinks he eats enough (I'nʌf)

no matter how much he eats.

He is sensitive to Roy's cough (kɒf).

It seems it can rack up his nerve (nɜːv).

But he is always eager to serve (sɜːv).

He picks shoes or newspaper for Roy.

He really can perform various tasks fairly well.

He always thinks himself a servant to Roy.

He thinks he has to perform (/ pə'fɔːm /)

seven ('sevn) duties daily to be deemed fit (fɪt).

| Consonant pair | [ ph ] | / f v / | 139 |

Mick laughs a lot every day.

She likes to take photographs.

She is interested in the geography (/ dʒɪˈɒgrəfɪ /) subject.

She thinks physics is a hard subject for her.

She never understands much about philosophy (/ fəˈlɒsəfɪ /).

However, she is well-versed in modern technology (/ tekˈnɒlədʒɪ /).

She always heaves a sigh of relief

at the thought of her strong points

and her weaknesses.

She always feels consoled

that she does not need to sit for any test now

to prove her ability.

Her good performance in life

is a good proof of her ability.

| | / f / | | / v / |
|---|---|---|---|
| 1. | fan | / fæn / | van | / væn / |
| 2. | fain | / feɪn / | vain | / veɪn / |
| 3. | fast | / fɑːst / | vast | / vɑːst / |
| 4. | few | / fjuː / | view | / vjuː / |
| 5. | ferry | / ˈferɪ / | very | / ˈverɪ / |
| 6. | fine | / faɪn / | vine | / vaɪn / |
| 7. | file | / faɪl / | vile | / vaɪl / |
| 8. | leaf | / liːf / | leave | / liːv / |
| 9. | grief | / griːf / | grieve | / griːv / |
| 10. | proof | / pruːf / | prove | / pruːv / |
| 11. | safe | / seɪf / | save | / seɪv / |
| 12. | relief | / rɪˈliːf / | relieve | / rɪˈliːv / |

Soo (/ su: /) likes to go the zoo (/ zu: /).

She likes to see the seals there

with so much zeal.

She likes to look at the zebras, too

She thinks those zebras are lovely.

Today her parents are going

to bring her to the zoo.

She wishes the car

would zoom to the zoo soon.

Soo is fussy about her fuzzy-look pet cat called Nuzz. (/ nu:z /)

Nuzz, her fuzzy-look pet cat always follows her

wherever she goes.

Today, for sure, she will follow Soo to the zoo.

She always grooms Nuzz, her fuzzy-look pet cat well

so that she can hold and cuddle her more often.

| Consonant pair | [ s z ] | / s z / | 142 |
|---|---|---|---|

Sean and his sister, Jean like to go to the beach

to feel the sea breeze.

Jean's pet cat, Luzzy (/ ˈluːzɪ /) likes to follow her

wherever she goes.

But Luzzy is sensitive to sea breezes (/ ˈbriːzəz /).

She wheezes (/ ˈwiːzəz /) and freezes easily.

Jean thinks Luzzy needs a muzzle (/ ˈmʌzl /)

to keep her feel at ease.

Luzzy is curious about the zip on the muzzle.

She is also curious about the straw

when Jean has a sip to give herself a treat.

| Consonant pair | [ s z ] | / s z / | 143 |

Irene is down with chicken pox.

She has to stay

inside the bedroom all day long

to play with her toy fox in a box.

She has some toy crabs, lobsters, prawns,

squids and octopuses in another box (bɒks).

She has a toy horse, too.

Irene thinks it looks rather clumsy (/ 'klʌmzɪ /).

Irene is displaying her other toys

all over her bedroom.

She has fallen asleep now

and she is in the wonderland of toys.

| | / s / | | / z / | |
|---|---|---|---|---|
| 1. | soo | / suː / | zoo | / zuː / |
| 2. | seal | / siːl / | zeal | / ziːl / |
| 3. | soon | / suːn / | zoon | / zuːn / |
| 4. | fuss | / fʌs / | fuzz | / fʌz / |
| 5. | fussy | / 'fʌsɪ / | fuzzy | / 'fʌzɪ / |
| 6. | muscle | / 'mʌsl / | muzzle | / 'mʌzl / |
| 7. | *refuse | / re'fjuːs / | refuse | / rɪ'fjuːz / |
| 8. | abuse | / ə'bjuːs / | abuse | / ə'bjuːz / |
| 9. | sink | / sɪŋk / | zinc | / zɪŋk / |
| 10. | sip | / sɪp / | zip | / zɪp / |
| 11. | sing | / sɪŋ / | zing | / zɪŋ / |
| 12. | sap | / sæp / | zap | / zæp / |

Soo bathes (/ beɪðz /) her pet cat, Nuzz once a week.

Nuzz does not like to have a bath (/ bɑːθ /).

She finds it hard to breathe (/ briːð /).

She tends to hold her breath (/ breθ /)

when Soo bathes her.

Then Soo wipes her with a piece of cloth

before she helps her to put on some clothes.

Nuzz hates all these (ðiːz).

How she wishes (/ ˈwɪʃəz /) she could tell Soo the truth.

She has so little faith in water to keep clean.

She has her way

to keep herself spick and span.

She wishes Soo would leave her alone

and minds her own business.

| Consonant pairs | [ th ] | / θ ð / | 146 |
|---|---|---|---|

Sean's pet hamster Fine-I has given birth (/ bɜ:θ /)

to three little ones.

He wants to keep two hamsters, for sure.

He will give the third (θɜ:d) hamster to Jean, his sister.

He always reminds Jean, his sister

to take good care of the health (/ helθ /) of her hamster.

He always sees his hamster a kind of wealth (welθ) he has.

Sean likes to look at his hamsters

eating nuts, seeds and grains.

He thinks they really have strong teeth (ti:θ).

They could crack open any nuts

no matter how hard they are.

Sean wonders.

whether (/ 'weðə(r) /) they suffer any toothache.

| Consonant pair | [ th ] | / θ ð / | 147 |

Hed knows "Health is more important than wealth (welθ)."

He also thinks you just cannot buy health

with your wealth.

He knows he has to be in good health

to enjoy his life to the fullest.

He must listen to his mother (/ ˈmʌðə(r) /)

to exercise every day.

He will jog with his father (/ fɑːðə(r) /)

along the path (/ pɑːθ /) every morning or evening.

He thinks he should try to eat less bread.

But he knows it is not an easy thing to do.

Hed (/ hed /) feels hungry easily.

Instead of eating half a loaf of bread,

nowadays, he only has three slices a day.

He has (/ hæz /) to exercise a lot.

He helps (/ helps /) in the household chores (/ tʃɔːz /).

He feeds the hens for his mother

though he hates those hens a lot.

He always feels lazy and sleepy

when the weather is hot and humid ('hjuːmɪd).

He loses all his sense of humour (/ 'hjuːmə(r) /)

in such a condition of weather (/ 'weðə(r) /).

| Consonant | [ h ] | / h / | 149 |
|-----------|-------|-------|-----|

Hed feels humiliated (/ hju:'mɪlIeItId /)

when someone calls him 'Fatty Hed'.

He knows he looks fat and huge for his age.

But he thinks it is hard and harsh (/ hɑːʃ /)

to endure being teased in that manner.

He thinks he needs to discipline himself more.

He should climb up the hill at least once a week.

He should take part in hip-hop dance to slim down.

He can have hip-hop at home (/ həʊm /).

He can hit sandbags to trim off.

He can play hockey (/ 'hʊkI /) with his friends.

He should cultivate good habits (/ 'hæbIts /).

He really need some hobbies

to keep his mind off the food.

| / h / | / θ | ð / |
|---|---|
| | |
| 1. hat | that |
| 2. his | this |
| 3. health | |
| 4. wealth | |
| 5. hill | thrill |
| 6. hose | those |
| 7. *here | there |
| 8. high | thigh |
| 9. hen | then |

Minimal pair / t ----- θ | ð /

| / t / | / θ | ð / |
|---|---|
| | |
| 1. tree | three |
| 2. tread | thread |
| 3. tin | thin |
| 4. *toss / tɒs / | those / ðəʊz / |
| 5. ten | then |
| 6. taught | thought |
| 7. trill | thrill |
| 8. tank | thank |
| | |
| / θ / | / ð / |
| * breath / breθ / | breathe / briːð / |
| cloth / klɒθ / | clothes / kləʊðz / , / kləʊz / |

faith, truth,                                                    151

health, wealth

thank thaw, theatre

theme                              them

theory, thesis, thermo            father, mother, brother,

thin, thick, think, thing         this, that, these, those

thirsty, thirty, thought          then, they, them, though,

thorn, thousand, thrash           although,

thread, threat, three

Sean often prays

that it will not rain at weekends.

He wants to play

with Mark and others in the park.

They like to look around for rooks

and their broods.

They like to climb up a really big rock.

They always wonder

whether Magic Monkey in a Chinese story

was being locked up

under a rock bigger than this.

| Consonant pair | [ l r ] | / l r / | 153 |
|---|---|---|---|

Bip is really thin.

Sean always thinks

that he must be very light, too.

He sometimes wonders

if a very strong wind would blow him

right up into the sky.

Well, Bip always can leap higher than many.

He reaps most in high jump

and long jump events.

He collects most trophies among them all.

Sean always thinks he is correct.

that Bip is indeed thin and light.

Most of his friends also think that he is right.

| Consonant pair | [ l r ] | / l r / | 154 |

Once there was an old man.

He always wore a blue shirt (/ ʃɜːt /)

and a pair of brown shorts. (/ ʃɔːt /)

He liked to brew some tea in the evening

when the wind blew hard.

Then he drank a glass (/ glɑːs /) of tea,

sitting on the grass (grɑːs).

His two bright (braɪt) eyes seemed

to sparkle so much at night.

His face glowed as much in the light (laɪt).

He liked to grow some beans

and peas in his garden.

At times, he related the plight

he endured in life.

It was rife with rumours

that he had some magic power

and was very wise.

| Consonant pair | [ l r ] | / l r / | 155 |

Sean knows it is wrong (/ rɒŋ /)

to watch television all day long (/ lɒŋ /).

He feels low (/ ləʊ /)

whenever he has a row (/ rəʊ /)

with someone he knows well or not.

He thinks he is too green and blunt.

Thus he has to bear the brunt

of being blunt.

His mind just goes bland

When he sees mice eating rice and lice.

He thinks he need a brand new mouse-trap

to catch mice.

He needs to get rid of lice, too.

He can use the garbage enzyme

in a can with a red lid to kill them all.

|  | / l / | | / r / | |
|---|---|---|---|---|
| 1. | lag | / læg / | rag | / ræg / |
| 2. | lap | / læp / | rap | / ræp / |
| 3. | lay | / leɪ / | ray | / reɪ / |
| 4. | led | / led / | red | / red / |
| 5. | lid | / lɪd / | rid | / rɪd / |
| 6. | life | / laɪf / | rife | / raɪf / |
| 7. | light | / laɪt / | right | / raɪt / |
| 8. | link | / lɪŋk / | rink | / rɪŋk / |
| 9. | loss | * / lɒs / | rose | * / rəʊz / |
| 10. | low | / ləʊ / | row | / rəʊ / |
| 11. | lace | / leɪs / | race | / reɪs / |
| 12. | laid | / leɪd / | raid | / reɪd / |
| 13. | lain | / leɪn / | rain | / reɪn / |
| 14. | leap | / liːp / | reap | / riːp / |
| 15. | lent | / lent / | rent | / rent / |
| 16. | lice | / laɪs / | rice | / raɪs / |
| 17. | long | / lɒŋ / | wrong | / rɒŋ / |
| 18. | load | / ləʊd / | road | / rəʊd / |
| 19. | look | / luk / | rook | / ruk / |
| 20. | lock | / lɒk / | rock | / rɒk / |
| 21. | luck | / lʌk / | ruck | / rʌk / |
| 22. | lust | / lʌst / | rust | / rʌst / |
| 23. | bland | / blænd / | brand | / brænd / |

| 24. | blight | / blaɪt / | bright | / braɪt / | 157 |
|-----|--------|-----------|--------|-----------|-----|
| 25. | block | / blɒk / | brock | / brɒk / | |
| 27. | blunt | / blʌnt / | brunt | / brʌnt / | |
| 28. | glass | / glɑːs / | grass | / grɑːs / | |
| 29. | glow | / gləʊ / | grow | / grəʊ / | |
| 30. | collect | / kəˈlekt / | correct | / kəˈrekt / | |
| 31. | play | / pleɪ / | pray | / preɪ / | |

Mark likes to help his mother,

Mdm Ma to make a mango cake.

His ambition is to become a baker

or a chef or a computer technician.

He thinks he would like to be

a part-time magician.

But his mum always says,

"You must know how

to manage your time to become efficient.

Then you will lead a more meaningful,

interesting and happy life."

Mark knows he has to study hard and be smart.

He must read widely and a lot

to become a well-informed and a well-versed person.

Yes, he must be well-prepared

to fulfil his ambition and mission in life.

| Consonant | [ m ] | / m / | 159 |
|---|---|---|---|

Mark, Mary and Tim are bothers and sister.

They like to have merry-making and games

under the coconut palms (/ pɑːmz /).

They really enjoy themselves so much.

Mdm Ma, their mum does not mind

if they are smeared with dirt and mud.

She sees it no harm and never feels alarmed.

She always keeps cool and calm

to see the mud or mess all over the place.

She makes no comment (/ ˈkɒmənt /) no matter how.

She only watches out so as to make sure

that they follow the rules

and adopt the correct manners (/ ˈmænəz /).

"Oh, no! The wind is blowing on and on,"

laments Noh-on, the farmer.

He has never seen the wind blowing

in this manner.

It has been blowing for almost a month.

The crops he has grown just sways

and bends so much.

Noh-on and Hon-on, his wife are nervous and upset.

They wonder if the wind would ever stop again (/ əˈgeɪn /)

and come back to normal.

If the wind blows in this manner once in a while,

it could be fun, for sure.

You certainly could enjoy the windy (/ ˈwɪndɪ /) day.

You could indulge in kite-flying

But this wind is threatening

to his livelihood and good living (/ ˈlɪvɪŋ /).

Remember the letter "n" in "ng or nk" will change into / ŋ / speech sound. When the words that end in "ng", the phoneme / g / is almost always dropped like [ sing, wing, king, fling, ……. ]. But for the word "En-glish", the phoneme / g / sound is articulated in the second syllable " / ˈɪŋglɪʃ / ".

Sean enjoys swimming in a river.

He always brings along his swimming trunks.

When he swims,

he always clings to a square board.

He wishes he would swim all day long

and far beyond.

When he is tired with swimming,

he would rest under a tree beside a tank.

He would like to wander

along the bank with his family.

They always look out for wasps (/ wɒsps /)

as the sting of them can be fatal

and can cause so much pain.

| 48. Consonants in comparison | / n ŋ / |
|---|---|

| / n / | / ŋ / (ng / nk) | 162 |
|---|---|---|

| | / n / | / ŋ / (ng / nk) |
|---|---|---|
| 1. | san / sæn / | sang / sæŋ / |
| 2. | sin / sɪn / | sing / sɪŋ / |
| 3. | * son / sʌn / | song / sɒŋ / |
| 4. | pin / pɪn / | ping / pɪŋ / |
| 5. | tan / tæn / | tang / tæŋ / \| tank / tæŋk / |
| 6. | ton / tʌn / | tongs / tɒŋz / |
| 7. | than / ðæn / | thank / θæŋk / |
| 8. | thin / θɪn / | think / θɪŋk / \| thing / θɪŋ / |
| 9. | brine / braɪn / | bring / brɪŋ / |
| 10. | alone * / əˈləʊn / | along * / əˈlɒŋ / |

The letter cluster 'ng' is almost released as / ŋ / in speech sound whereas the letter cluster 'nk' is always released as / ŋk / in speech sound.

Ozee likes to listen to a story about a queen

who was very quiet ('kwaɪət).

Many courtiers (kɔ:tɪəz) who (/ hu: /) did not know her well (/ wel /)

wondered whether she was deaf and dumb.

She kept a pet quail (/ kweɪl /) called Quay (/ ki: /)

and a squirrel (/ 'skwɪrəl /) called Bouquet (/ bʊ'keɪ /).

She knew how to make a square (skweə(r)) quilt (/ kwɪlt /) fairly well.

She never liked to powder her face white (waɪt) or pink.

She never drank wine (/ waɪn /) in her life.

She only wanted plain water (/ 'wɔ:tə(r) /) or tea.

She knows how to win

the heart of the king very well.

| Consonant | [ w ] | / w / | 164 |

Ozee always get wet

when she helps wash dishes.

The sink is far above her waist (/ weɪst /).

Olly, her mum always advises her to wait

until she is a bit taller.

She would rather wash (/ wɒʃ /) dishes

than watch (wɒtʃ) television.

She thinks it fun to play with water (/ 'wɔ:t(r) /)

while (/ waɪl /) she is washing dishes.

Mdm Chan likes to make cucumber, turnip

and pineapple salad for dinner.

Yoyo (/ ˈjəujəu /), her pet cat always meows

and yawns (/ jɔ:nz /) so much at her feet.

She always meows for a favour of a huge (/ hju:dʒ /) fish.

When Mdm Chan yells, "Wait!",

all her yellow (/ ˈjeləʊ /) fur just stands stiff in fright.

Yoyo feels humiliated a little bit.

She curls up in U-shape

and waits for the cue (/ kju: /) for a huge (/ hju:dʒ /) fish.

| Consonant | [ y ] | / j / | 166 |

Sean's cousin Yong-yo ('jɒŋjəu) is a hardworking young (/ jʌŋ /) man.

He is strong and healthy, too.

He is a youth (/ ju:θ /) with a promising future ('fju:tʃə).

He knows there are a few things

he must do to fulfil his ambition and mission in life.

He must know his aptitude (/ 'æptɪtju:d /) to develop himself.

He thinks forming good habits is important, too.

Besides, he knows he must have

his own point of view (/ vju: /) to stay unique (/ ju'ni:k /).

He always thinks hard

before he answers any Yes- No questions.

He must always upkeep himself

with new (/ nju: /) knowledge and skill as well.

Once there was a queen called Queen Quest (/ kwest /).

She was quite (/ kwaɪt /) quiet (/ ˈkwaɪət /).

But at times she could be quite talkative

and inquisitive *(/ ɪŋˈkwɪzətɪv /).

She likes to ask Wh-questions to enquire *(/ ɪŋˈkwaɪə(r) /)

to ease her curiosity (/ ˌkjʊərɪˈɒsətɪ /) about things.

She was queer (/ kwɪə(r) /) in this respect

though she knew, "Curiosity kills the cat."

However, she never squabbled (/ skwɒbld /) with anybody in her life.

Just in case there was a squabble

between her chambermaids,

she would think of all ways to quell (/ kwel /) the quarrel. (ˈkwɒrəl)

She never quibbled (/ ˈkwɪbld /) over anything with anybody.

She was only interested in acquiring knowledge (/ ˈnɒlɪdʒ /)

and skill to be qualified as a queen.

She cared to uphold the quality of life.

She remembered her mother's advice,

"We should live a high quality (ˈkwɒlətɪ) life

and give a high quantity (/ ˈkwɒntətɪ /) love."

| Consonants | [ qu ] | / kw /, / k / | 168 |

Quoguo (/ ˈkwəugəu /) is a self-disciplined

and self-willed boy.

Though he has high emotional quotient (/ ˈkwəuʃnt /),

he still quivers (/ ˈkwɪvə(r) /) and quavers (/ ˈkweɪvəz /) at times.

When he performs in a quartet (/ kwɔːˈtet /) or quintet (/ kwɪnˈtet /)

in a show,

he always faces some initial hiccup.

Nevertheless, he quickly conquers (/ ˈkɒŋkəz /) his fear.

Que, Quoguo's mum always quips saying

that the fear is just quotidian (/ kwɒˈtɪdɪən /)

every performer has to squash.

Que, Quoguo's mum always advises him

to memorise some quotations to quit the qualm.

She always reminds him, not to squirm nor squint

but stay calm at all times.

Mdm Chan, Sean's mum has bought him

a brand new wrist watch.

It was water-proof and automatic.

Sean likes it very much.

He wears it to school.

He wears it to bed.

It is unique though it looks like a duplicate ('dju:plIkeIt)

of his dad's old watch.

The watch, Dr. Vet used to wear in his youth

when he went around on duty (/ 'dju:tI /).

There are few (/ fju: /) of this kind around nowadays

The front view (/ vju: /) of Sean's watch is very attractive.

Jean likes Sean's watch, too.

But Sean refuses (/ rI'fju:zəz /) to lend her

to wear just for a while.

To pacify Jean, Mdm Chan gave her

the old watch to wear.

Dr. Vet is amused (ə'mju:zd) at the sight

when Jean wears the old watch to school, too.